Ten Principles of Regulation & Reform

Darren Brady Nelson

LibertyFest, Brisbane
Monograph 2

Connor Court Publishing

Published in 2017 by Connor Court Publishing

Copyright © Darren Brady Nelson

Connor Court Publishing Pty Ltd
PO Box 7257
Redland Bay QLD 4165
sales@connorcourt.com
www.connorcourt.com

Phone 0497 900 685

ISBN: 978-1-925501-68-1

Cover design: Maria Giordano

Printed in Australia

Distributed in Australia by Brumby SunState and Connor Court Publishing

Distributed in the UK, Europe, and North America by Ingram Inc.

LibertyFest Monographs

LibertyFest is conceived as a series of annual conferences celebrating and honouring the very idea of liberty. Ideas such as all individuals being free to enjoy their natural rights to life, liberty and property. That each of us should be free to live our lives in the manner that suits us provided we respect the equal rights of others to do the same. The idea that the rule of common law and enforcement can be used to protect people's natural rights but that state enforcement should not be used to coerce people into things they do not care for. The idea that we each have the ability to exercise free will and in doing so will take responsibility for the consequences of our actions.

These ideas are not new, they emerged from the writings of classical liberal economists and libertarian philosophers over many centuries. However, in recent times these ideas are gradually being eroded and diluted as interventionist fads take hold at both a governmental level and among the voting public. The arguments for free markets, smaller government and less tax are having to be remade to new generations which is why Connor Court and LibertyFest have created the LibertyFest Series of Monographs drawn from selected LibertyFest speakers.

Ten Principles of Regulation & Reform is our second Monograph in this series, written by Austrian School economist Darren Nelson. Darren has increasingly devoted his time and efforts to the economics and ethics of liberty in Australia, the UK and the USA. During this time he has increasingly drawn from the real-world-based Austrian School of economics, whilst retaining the best of the other schools like Chicago and Virginia. In this time, Darren has done work as a sole trader for such outfits as: Americans for Tax Reform; Center for Freedom and Prosperity; Crime Prevention Research Center; Friedman Conference; Frontiers of Freedom; Grade Gov; Heartland Institute; Liberal National Party; MacIver Institute; Master Resource; Mises Canada; Mises Institute; Tea Party Australia; Tea Party USA; Terabit Media; Townhall; Townhall Finance; Utility Week; Wisconsin Manufacturing & Commerce; and LibertyWorks.

LibertyFest conferences exist to give a voice and a forum for liberty loving ideas. When you read this book and attend a LibertyFest conference our hope is you do this with an open mind. Open to learning something new and being prepared to shoulder a small amount of responsibility to help spread these ideas among your friends. The future may depend upon it.

Andrew Cooper, Director

LibertyFest, Brisbane

TABLE OF CONTENTS

Introduction

"Government is not a solution to our problem,
government is the problem!"

–President Ronald Reagan

Lawyers tend to define regulation narrowly as either subsidiary legislation from the legislative branch of government and/or legal instruments from the executive branch of government. Economists tend to define regulation broadly as those government interventions or interferences in the economy that are not taxation, expenditure or money printing. This includes the lawyers definition above plus any primary legislation as well as judicial interpretation or creation of laws. The latter **definition** is adopted here. It is sometimes referred to as 'red tape', which can include environmental 'green tape' and international or UN 'blue tape'.

Money **inflation** mainly drives price inflation, as well as facilitates government inflation like taxation and regulation. Taxation and regulation adds to price inflation mainly through: a) reducing efficient supply and competition – ie a shortage from eg a tax or a price ceiling regulation; and/or b) increasing inefficient supply and entry – ie a surplus from eg a subsidy or a price floor regulation (see the two graphs below). Both also hide behind money inflation by say increasing: hidden taxation through income bracket creep; or the use of price ceiling regulations to supposedly deal with price inflation.

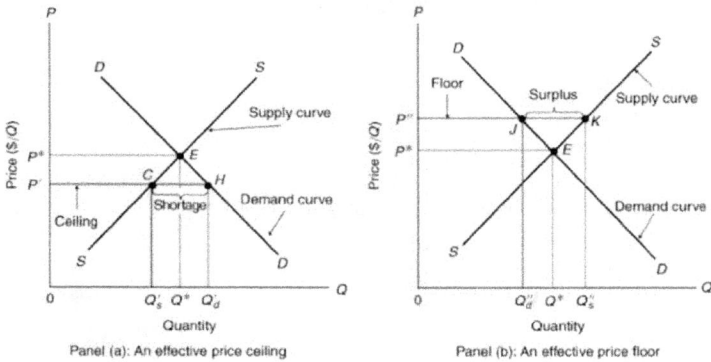

Panel (a): An effective price ceiling — Panel (b): An effective price floor

{Hirshleifer 2005}

Federal or Commonwealth red tape in **Australia** is very high and has been steadily accumulating since 1901 (see the first graph below). There is some cause for hope as the annual growth, of both legislation and subsidiary legislation, has been trending downwards since the early 1990s (see the second graph below). {Nelson 2017}

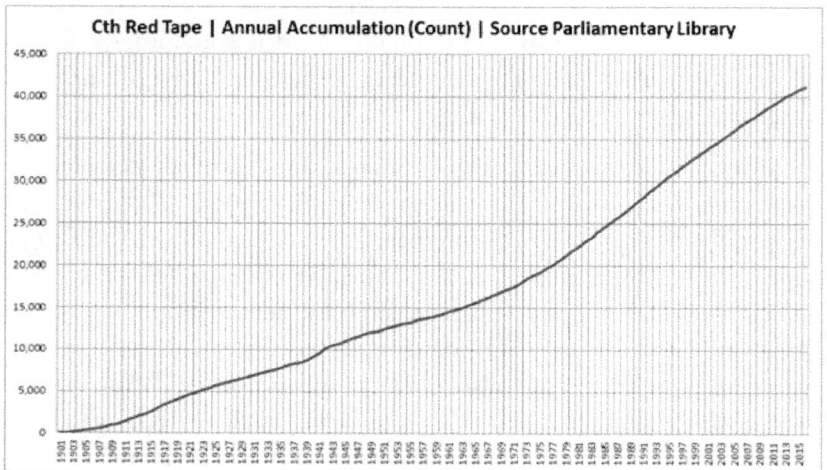

Cth Red Tape | Annual Accumulation (Count) | Source Parliamentary Library

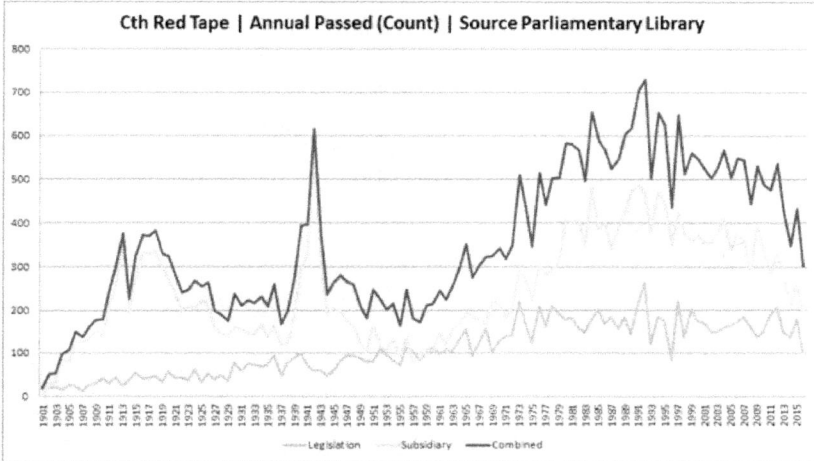

Cth Red Tape | Annual Passed (Count) | Source Parliamentary Library

The Competitive Enterprise Institute (CEI) has been estimating the **costs** of regulation every year for the USA since 1996 in a publication entitled *Ten Thousand Commandments*. In the 2017 edition, for example, it was stated that: "If one assumed that all costs of federal regulation and intervention flowed all the way down to households, [they] would 'pay' $14,809 annually on average in a regulatory hidden tax. That amounts to 21% of the average income of $69,629 and 26% of the expenditure budget of $55,978. The 'tax' exceeds every item in the budget except housing. More is 'spent' on embedded regulation than on health care, food, transportation, entertainment, apparel, services, and savings.". {Crews 2017} The situation in Australia is similar, if not worse. One indicator of this is, as any sound economist would expect, CPI for the lightly regulated goods and services is falling whilst that for the heavily regulated ones is rising (see the first graph below). The 'poster child' for the latter is electricity (see the second graph below). {Nelson 2017}

CPI Heavily v Lightly Regulated | Dec-on-Dec Accumulation (Index) | Source ABS

CPI All v Electricity | Dec-on-Dec Accumulation (Index 100) | Source ABS

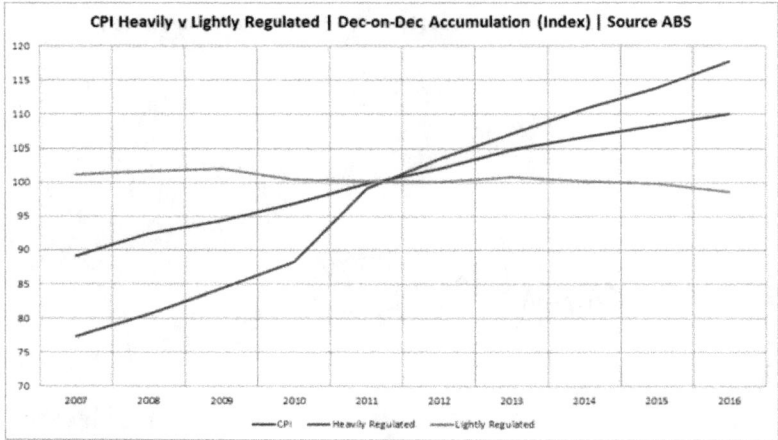

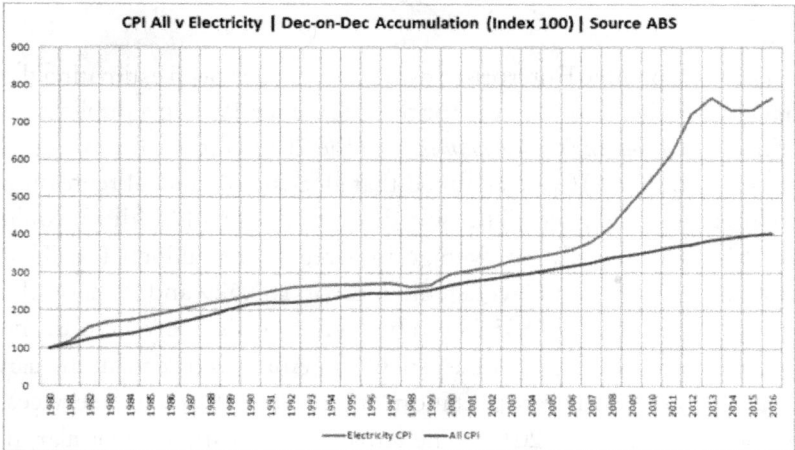

Deregulation, better/smarter regulation and other regulation **reforms** have certainly been tried and tested, to varying degrees and successes over a number of decades in Australia, the USA and around-the-world. The main approaches have traditionally included: embedded in-and-out and sunset provisions; one-off audits or reviews; ongoing executive, legislative or judicial review; regular regulatory impact assessments, cost benefit analysis or business compliance cost calculators; as well as simple budgetary restrictions or bureaucratic inefficiency and ineffectiveness.

One crucial point to note upfront is that value is always subjective to each individual at any one point in time and, thus, there are no unambiguous and objective opportunity costs and benefits of regulations as a whole that can readily be observed, calculated and compared. Nevertheless, it is still important to try to better understand regulation and its burdens on businesses, consumers and taxpayers through some sort of rigorous **measurement** and quantification ... but as informed and guided by sound economic logic and policy principles. The main tools have traditionally included: counts of ... all or just command words, instruments, pages, public and private sector regulatory employment; cost-benefit analysis; and opinion surveys. However, regulation does not readily lend itself to measurement and quantification like other mechanisms of government intervention do such as taxation and subsidisation, and thus it is harder to understand the magnitude and even the exact nature of the almost infinite potential problems caused-and-effected by regulation. This is particularly the case with the ongoing, and ever evolving, unintended negative consequences of regulation.

A second crucial point to note upfront is that there is usually some combination of 'true believers and special interests' to the origination, continuation and growth of regulation. This was colourfully dubbed by Bruce Yandle as the '**baptists and bootleggers**' phenomenon. "Yandle observed that unvarnished special interest groups cannot expect politicians to push through legislation [or regulation] that simply raises prices on a few products so that the protected group can get rich at the expense of consumers. Like the bootleggers in the early-20th-century South, who benefited from laws that banned the sale of liquor on Sundays, special interests need to justify their efforts to obtain special favors with public interest stories. In the case of Sunday liquor sales, the Baptists, who supported the Sunday ban on moral grounds, provided that public interest support. While the Baptists vocally endorsed the ban on Sunday sales, the bootleggers worked behind the scenes and quietly rewarded the politicians with a portion of their Sunday liquor sale profits." {Dudley & Brito 2012}

A third crucial point to note upfront is that, when it comes to future regulation, legislators and regulation-makers (and even economists) would do well to always heed the warnings of Nobel Laureate Friedrich von Hayek about "a **pretense** of exact knowledge that is likely to be false". In other words: "To act on the belief that we possess the knowledge and the power which enable us to shape the processes of society entirely to our liking, knowledge which in fact we do not possess, is likely to make us do much harm." Thus, he concluded: "If man is not to do more harm than good in his efforts to improve the social order, he will have to learn that in this, as in all other fields where essential complexity of an organized kind prevails, he cannot acquire the full knowledge which would make mastery of the events possible." {Hayek 1974}

It is certainly self-evident that sound principles are needed to help guide better understanding and public policy making going forward. *The Ten Principles of Regulation and Reform*, to be discussed at length in the coming pages, therefore are such a guide. Note that each of the following chapters are broadly structured as follows:

- What is this principle exactly?

- Why is this principle important?

- How is this principle applied?

References:

- Darren Brady Nelson, *The Cost-of-Living: The Evidence is Clear*, 2017

- Friedrich von Hayek, *The Pretence of Knowledge*, 1974

- Jack Hirshleifer & et al, *Price Theory and Applications*, 2005

- Susan Dudley & Jerry Brito, *Regulation: A Primer*, 2012

- Wayne Crews, *Ten Thousand Commandments*, 2017

Principles

1. Regulations seldom solve problems

Regulations in the shorter term may help a relatively small group of individuals at the expense of everybody else, but won't even help the former in the longer term without further regulations at the increasing expense of all.

Depending on whose viewpoint, regulations may be able to solve **problems** (that are usually the result of previous regulations). Too often these regulations are cloaked in the public interest when in fact they were intended only for a relatively small group of private interests. Even when that was not the true intention of legislators and regulation-makers, such regulations invariably still have largely negative unintended consequences, for which yet further regulations are called for and so on. To paraphrase economist Ludwig von Mises who nicely summed up the issue: "[Regulation] is a self-defeating policy. The individual measures that it applies do not achieve the results sought. They bring about a state of affairs, which – from the viewpoint of its advocates themselves – is much more undesirable than the previous state they intended to alter." {Mises 1944}

From a Public Choice Theory (**PCT**) perspective, the regulation problem is essentially one of government failure. Susan Dudley and Jerry Brito of the Mercatus Center put the theory this way: "[PCT] recognizes that (1) individuals in government (politicians, regulators, voters, etc) are driven by self-interest, just as individuals in other circumstances are, and (2) they are not omniscient." And furthermore: "[PCT] is concerned with the economic waste inherent in efforts to change laws or regulations in order to privilege one group over another. Such activity is called rent-seeking." And particularly relevant to regulation is that: "[PCT] recognizes that policymakers cannot always predict the consequences of different policy choices, so market interventions may produce government failures. That is, even when a market failure is observed, a particular government intervention may produce even more inefficiency than the *status quo* as a result of the rent-seeking problem, unintended consequences, or both." Worse still, according to Dudley and Brito: "[S]pecial interests are disinclined to seek direct wealth transfers because their machinations would be too obvious. Instead, regulatory approaches that purport to provide public benefits confuse the public and reduce voter opposition to transfers of wealth to special interests." {Dudley & Brito 2012}

From an Austrian School Economics (**ASE**) perspective, the regulation problem is essentially one of economic calculation. Mises originated this and said thusly that: "Without market prices for the means of production, government planners cannot engage in economic calculation, and so literally have no idea if they are using society's resources efficiently. Consequently, socialism [and interventionism] suffers not only from a problem of incentives, but also from a problem of knowledge." {Mises 1932} Robert Murphy of the Institute of Energy Research succinctly adds from an ASE perspective that: "To match the performance of a market economy, [legislators and regulation-makers] would not need to be merely angels, committed to the commonweal – they would also need to be gods, capable of superhuman calculations." {Murphy 2010}

Mises expanded on the importance of another issue for both the regulators and the regulated – ie **bureaucracy**: "[T]he whole character of their management changes. They are no longer eager to deal with each case to the best of their abilities; they are no longer anxious to find the most appropriate solution for every problem. Their main concern is to comply with the regulations, no matter whether they are reasonable or contrary to what was intended. The first virtue of an administrator is to abide by the codes and decrees. He becomes a bureaucrat." Bureaucracy is the antithesis of problem-solving and consumer-driven entrepreneurialism. In this regard, Mises went on to point out that: "[The bureaucratic] deficiencies and faults of the management of administrative agencies are necessary properties." This is always and everywhere because: "A bureau is not a profit-seeking enterprise; it cannot make use of any economic calculation." Unfortunately, therefore: "It is out of the question to improve its management by reshaping it according to the pattern of private business." And this inevitably leads to regulatory failure, even though: "The failure … was certainly not due to incapacities of the personnel. It was an outcome of the unavoidable weakness of any administration of public affairs [ie] [t]he lack of [profit-and-loss, price and customer oriented] standards [which] kills ambition, destroys initiative and the incentive to do more than the minimum required. It makes the bureaucrat look at instructions, not at material and real success." {Mises 1944}

All of these issues are obviously important and lend further credence to looking to free and competitive markets to solve problems … most likely problems created by regulations in the first place or at least those that were tried subsequently to rectify, perhaps in many subsequent rounds. At a still deeper level, regulatory **failure** often occurs as "statesmen and public officials, no matter how powerful they may be, cannot finally control social outcomes" because these are ultimately "shaped by human actions, stemming from imaginative human minds working out individual subjective valuations, and their interactions with the material world, which is governed by [economic] laws that are beyond human control". This is according to the founder and president of the Mises Institute, Llewellyn Rockwell, who adds that: "There is no magic solution to getting around basic economic laws. All lunches must be paid for by someone, prices cannot be both high and low at the same time, and all attempts to coerce generate counter-reactions. In short, there is no alternative universe [for regulators to simply do as they please] ..." {Rockwell 2008}

A classic example of **harmful** regulations are minimum wage and other pro labour union ones. In this regard, economist Milton Friedman highlighted that: "[T]he ability of unions to raise the wages of some workers does not mean that universal unionism could raise the wages of all workers. On the contrary, and this is a fundamental source of misunderstanding, the gains that strong unions win for their members are primarily at the expense of other workers." And: "The key to understanding the situation is the most elementary principle of economics: the law of demand – [m]ake labor of any kind more expensive and the number of jobs of that kind will be fewer." {Friedman 1979} His son and fellow economist David Friedman provides a less obvious example of harmful regulations – ie. "Physicians justify restricting the number of physicians, to others and doubtless to themselves as well, on the grounds of keeping up quality." But: "Even if that were really what they were doing, the argument involves a fundamental error. Refusing to license the less qualified 50% of physicians may raise the average quality of physicians but it lowers the average quality of medical care." Therefore: "It does not mean that everyone gets better medical care but that half the people get no care or that everyone gets half as much." {Friedman 1989}

Australia has often been a transparent country to look to over the past few decades for world best practice in microeconomic **reforms**, including just copying and improving upon the reforms of other countries like the USA, UK and New Zealand. Regulation is one of those reforms. For decades, the Productivity Commission (PC) has undertaken regular reviews of existing regulations and industries for the Australian Government, regardless of ruling political party, including whether regulations are solving problems or not. For years, the Office of Best Practice Regulation (OBPR) has undertaken ongoing reviews of existing and proposed regulations utilising its business cost calculator (BCC), cost benefit analysis (CBA) and regulatory impact statements (RIS)… the latter which includes whether regulations are solving problems or not. More recently, there has been a Reducing Red Tape policy which includes acknowledgement of: "Regulatory failure"; "Keeping risk in perspective"; "Not every problem can be solved by government"; "The most important policy option: the no-regulation option"; and "Alternative instruments".

References:

- David Friedman, *Machinery of Freedom: Guide to a Radical Capitalism*, 1989

- Llewellyn Rockwell, *The Left, the Right, and the State*, 2008

- Ludwig von Mises, *Bureaucracy*, 1944

- Ludwig von Mises, *Socialism: An Economic and Sociological Analysis*, 1932

- Milton & Rose Friedman, *Free To Choose: A Personal Statement*, 1979

- Robert Murphy, *Chaos Theory*, 2010

- Susan Dudley & Jerry Brito, *Regulation: A Primer*, 2012

2. Beware of unintended consequences

Legislators and regulation-makers should always be aware that unintended negative consequences of regulation are more than likely to eventually outweigh the intended positive ones, which cannot usually be fixed through risking yet more of the former.

It should be noted that what was **intended** or not by legislators and regulation-makers are an important and interesting area of thought and examination. For example, whether or not these, from the viewpoints of the regulators, regulated and others, were achieved and positive, and to what degree, when, where, how, why, etc. Arguably more important and interesting are the consequences themselves whether intended or not, particularly as these tend to be negative, less tangible and much larger. These are like the submerged part of the regulatory burden iceberg, rather than the tip above the surface. The more tangible burdens are a quite manageable list of the more immediate impacts such as extra money spent by business to comply and government to enforce regulation. The less tangible burdens are an almost infinite list of the less immediate impacts, such as lower performance throughout the economy in terms of entrepreneurship, innovation, growth, supply quantities and quality, prices, customer service, jobs, etc.

In Austrian economist Robert Bradley's regulation **dynamics** typology, he notes: "A match of intention and result equates to success for the involved political entrepreneurs." But that: "Unintended consequences have been a hallmark of interventionism due to complexity of policymaking where everything is related to everything else." Thus: "Three categories within unintended consequences can be distinguished: predictable; unpredicted; and unpredictable. The predicable consequences of an intervention are those that can be reasonably foreseen from an understanding of interventionism. Other unintended consequences may be less predictable *ex ante* but understandable *ex post*." In addition: "[G]aming [can] defeat the aims of regulators despite their best efforts to prevent it. [This] creates potential for [regulator] learning to do better next time in analogous situations." But: "The deeper the cumulative process, the more unintended and unforeseen the regulatory process becomes. At some point the unforeseen turns into the unforeseeable; the total surprise that is so unique that it is beyond what could have learned through past experience." {Bradley 2003}

The father of the idea of **unintended** consequences is politically economy writer Claude Frédéric Bastiat who identified that: "In the economy... a law, gives birth not only to an effect, but to a series of effects. Of these effects, the first only is immediate; it manifests itself simultaneously with its cause – it is seen. The others unfold in succession – they are not seen." And: "Between a good and a bad economist this constitutes the whole difference – the one takes account of the visible effect; the other takes account both of the effects which are seen and also of those which it is necessary to foresee." Thus, in terms of regulation and other policies: "[I]t almost always happens that when the immediate consequence is favourable, the ultimate consequences are fatal, and the converse." {Bastiat 1850}

In talking about unintended consequences, economist Milton Friedman cleverly turned on its head the words of fellow economist Adam Smith about **self-interest** when he said: "In the government sphere, as in the market, there seems to be an invisible hand, but it operates in precisely the opposite direction from Adam Smith's: an individual who intends only to serve the public interest by fostering government intervention is led by an invisible hand to promote private interests, which was no part of his intention." {Friedman 1979} The unintended consequences of regulation are usually even worse than this, as they usually, unlike in free markets, promote a relatively small group of private interests at the expense of a relatively large group of individuals. This large group is often virtually everybody else, in less obvious but ever growing ways. And eventually it includes, somewhat ironically, coming back to bite the original beneficiaries.

Politically economy writer Henry Hazlitt echoed both Friedman and Bastiat when he lamented that: "In addition to these endless pleadings of self-interest, there is a second main factor that spawns new economic fallacies every day. This is the persistent tendency of men to see only the immediate effects of a given policy, or its effects only on a special group, and to neglect to inquire what the **long-run** effects of that policy will be not only on that special group but on all groups. ... In this lies almost the whole difference between good economics and bad." He then provided a simple policy lesson, that should also be followed by all legislators and regulation-makers, when he said: "[T]he whole of economics can be reduced to a single lesson, and that lesson can be reduced to a single sentence. The art of economics consists in looking not merely at the immediate but at the longer effects of any act or policy; it consists in tracing the consequences of that policy not merely for one group but for all groups." {Hazlitt 1946}

The better understanding and identification of the unintended negative consequences of regulation to the economy and society is very much less advanced and relatively under-served than that of say compliance and enforcement expenditures ... and certainly to that of government taxation, expenditure, bureaucracy, welfare, debt and even fiat money. Besides the use of such **tools** as CBA, much lateral thinking and trial-and-error will be needed going forward in thinking up and developing additional and even better tools and approaches of regulatory and reform analysis. All such tools and approaches must be guided by sound economic logic. Some of the best include: Bast 2010; Bradley 2003; Johnston 1996; Ikeda 1997; Kurrild-Klitgaard 2005; Mises 1929, 1932 & 1944; and Rothbard 1977. One of the main purposes of CBA is to better understand broader impacts like possible unintended consequences. This is mainly dealt with under CBA through shadow pricing. Shadow pricing is adjusting prices for, or creating prices from, failed or non-existent markets. Shadow pricing involves many techniques based on direct sources of information such as revealed or stated preferences as well as indirect sources of information such as related markets and studies, which are in turn based on direct sources. These include: benchmark world prices; contingent valuation; demonstrations; hedonic asset ricing; intermediate dose-response; partial valuation; plug-ins; preventative costs; replacement costs; and travel costs.

Perhaps nothing grabs and holds most people's interest, and teaches them better, than good **story** telling. Examples and case studies can perform this function in the world of non-fiction, and arguably none have done this better, when it comes to regulation, than: Contoski 1997 on health, safety, environment, natural resources, population, food, drugs and money; Friedman 1979 on trade, welfare, equality, schools, consumers, workers and money; and Rothbard 1977 on prices, cartels, licenses, standards, tariffs, immigration, wages, corporations, antitrust, conservation, patents, public utilities, eminent domain and money. The past of course can only help guide the possible future. So too, may fictional storytelling regarding that which is yet to come … say through a Wiki type database of descriptive examples and ideas of a less regulated and freer world. {Rand 1957}

References:

- Ayn Rand, *Atlas Shrugged*, 1957

- Claude Frédéric Bastiat, *That Which is Seen, and That Which is Not Seen*, 1850

- Edmund Contoski, *Makers and Takers: How Wealth and Progress Are Made and How They Are Taken Away or Prevented*, 1997

- Henry Hazlitt, *Economics in One Lesson*, 1946

- James Johnstone, *Which Industries Are Regulated?*, 1996

- Joe Bast, *Why Regulate? New Applications of the Johnston Test*, 2010

- Ludwig von Mises, *A Critique of Interventionism*, 1929

- Ludwig von Mises, *Bureaucracy*, 1944

- Ludwig von Mises, *Socialism: An Economic and Sociological Analysis*, 1932

- Milton & Rose Friedman, *Free To Choose: A Personal Statement*, 1979

- Murray Rothbard, *Power and Market: Government and the Economy*, 1977

- Peter Kurrild-Klitgaard (ed), *The Dynamics of Intervention: Regulation and Redistribution in the Mixed Economy*, 2005

- Robert Bradley, *A Typology of Interventionist Dynamics*, 2003

- Sanford Ikeda (ed), *Dynamics of the Mixed Economy: Toward a Theory of Interventionism*, 1997

3. Regulations frequently redistribute income and power

Markets have the voluntary power to create and distribute wealth, whereas regulations have only the power of force to redistribute and destroy wealth.

Sociologist Franz Oppenheimer was the first to so clearly distinguish the **political** from the economic when it came to power and income and the redistribution of these: "There are two fundamentally opposed means whereby man, requiring· sustenance, is impelled to obtain the necessary means for satisfying his desires. These are ... one's own labor and the forcible appropriation of the labor of others ... [and] I propose ... to call one's own labor and the equivalent exchange of one's own labor for the labor of others, the economic means for the satisfaction of needs, while the unrequited appropriation of the labor of others will be called the political means." He crucially added that: "[T]he contradiction consists only in the means by which the identical purpose, the acquisition of, economic objects of consumption, is to be obtained." And he thus warned: "Yet this is the critical point of the reasoning. ... This led [a thinker of the rank of Karl Marx] to designate slavery as an economic category, and force as an economic force – half truths which are far more dangerous than total untruths, since their discovery is more difficult, and false conclusions from them are inevitable." {Oppenheimer 1926}

Economist Murray Rothbard elaborated further on **power** and markets. He firstly acknowledged the common claim that: "The government should stand ready to employ its coercion to check or offset private coercion." He then explored the latter further: "A well-known type of private coercion is the vague but ominous-sounding economic power ... [but] [e]conomic power ... is simply the right under freedom to refuse to make an exchange. Every man has [and should have] this power." Thus, in terms of government regulation: "If we choose the economic power concept, we must employ violence to combat any refusal of exchange; if we reject it, we employ violence to prevent any violent imposition of exchange. There is no way to escape this either-or choice." And therefore: "What would be the consequence of adopting the economic power premise? It would be a society ... where the overt initiators of violence would be treated with kindness, while their victims would be upbraided as being really responsible for their own plight. Such a society would be truly a war of all against all." {Rothbard 1977}

Often those pushing for more regulation implicitly assume that the economic **pie** is either fixed and that they just want to get their fair share ... or that the economic pie does grow, but that regulation can still get them their fair share without any or minimal impact on its future growth. Both assumptions are wrong. This pie will grow if not overly interfered with, but can grow at a minimal rate, stall or even shrink due to excessive government intervention in markets including regulation. It is worth mentioning that there are those political elites who know that markets drive pie growth and can be harmed by their regulations, but don't care or even want that to happen because they don't approve of too much wealth or consumption by others. This is using their political power like regulation to redistribute and lower others income as the end in itself. This is obviously quite different from trying to correct so called market failures as the end for regulation, where redistribution is a means or just an outcome to be accepted.

In a simple yet brilliant bit of analysis, economist Milton Friedman, showed why political redistribution, through regulation or any other government mechanism, doesn't really work – ie **incentives** matter, when it comes to the size and distribution of the economic pie: "When you spend, you may spend your own money or someone else's; and you may spend for the benefit of yourself or someone else. Combining these two pairs of alternatives gives four possibilities. Category I in the table refers to your spending your own money on yourself. You clearly have a strong incentive both to economize and to get as much value as you can for each dollar you do spend. Category II refers to your spending your own money on someone else. You have the same incentive to economize as in Category I but not the same incentive to get full value for your money. Category III refers to your spending someone else's money on yourself. You have no strong incentive to keep down the cost, but you do have a strong incentive to get your money's worth. Category IV refers to your spending someone else's money on still another person. You have little incentive either to economize or to try to get … value most highly." {Friedman 1979}

YOU ARE THE SPENDER

On Whom Spent

Whose Money	You	Someone Else
Yours	I	II
Someone Else's	III	IV

There are a plethora of real world instances of regulatory **redistribution**. Economist George Reisman analyses a number of these including taxicabs. According to him: "The New York City taxicab industry provides a good example of the monopolistic protection of the inefficient many against the competition of the more efficient few." Such: "Licensing laws create monopolies by virtue of initiating force to reserve markets to the exclusive possession of the license holders." And thus: "Their effect is always to deprive the buyers of services they could have had, to raise the price of the services they are allowed to receive, to elevate the incomes of the license holders, and to depress the incomes of those who are excluded from the licensed fields and forced to crowd into other, less-well-paying fields." He importantly added that: "It may well be the case that licensing sometimes does serve, as its supporters often claim, to raise the minimum level of competence and expertise in a field and thus to guarantee to the buyers a higher level of service than they would have received in its absence. But even if this is true, it is not by any means an advantage to the buyers. It merely means, in many cases, that buyers are forced to buy a higher level of service than they want or need and, if they cannot afford the higher level of service, are forced to do without the service they could have had." {Reisman 1998}

Economist Gordon Tullock "was the first to appreciate the **trap** that regulation creates for future attempts to deregulate", especially without further redistributive regulations. Regarding this "Transitional Gains Trap", he noted that: "[R]egulated firms often are not unusually profitable, even in industries (such as taxicabs) where entry is explicitly limited and prices set at supra-competitive levels." That is: "This seeming anomaly occurs because markets capitalize the discounted present value of regulatory rents into current firm values." And hence: "Gains to the first group of owners are merely transitional; later owners' gains are zero." The implication then for deregulation is that: "These costs are the flip side of the rent-seeking costs. Just as the first generation of firm owners expended resources to obtain rents from regulation, so will subsequent generations of owners spend resources to avoid deregulation." In other words: "[D]eregulation may be socially beneficial overall, but it is not universally beneficial. The gross gains from deregulation must be netted out against the costs that current firm owners will bear to avoid losing regulation." And moving forward: "[W]e could presumably compensate the present beneficiaries; but the political possibilities seem … to be very small." {McChesney 1999}

Note that distribution sometimes comes into play using **tools** such as CBA, both what is likely and what should be, the latter using weightings. Also note that economic power sometimes comes into play in antitrust proceedings. The Lerner Index for example tries to measure market power through the gap between price and marginal cost. Marginal cost for one is nearly impossible to measure precisely on an ongoing basis at a reasonable cost, and it is also a major problem in measuring predatory pricing when price is supposedly below marginal cost.

References:

- Franz Oppenheimer, *The State: Its History and Development Viewed Sociologically*, 1926

- Fred McChesney, *Of Stranded Costs and Stranded Hopes The Difficulties of Deregulation*, 1999

- George Reisman, *Capitalism: A Treatise on Economics*, 1998

- Milton & Rose Friedman, *Free To Choose: A Personal Statement*, 1979

- Murray Rothbard, *Power and Market: Government and the Economy*, 1977

4. Few regulations are actually intended to protect consumers

Many regulations are publicly stated to protect consumers, but not many are privately intended to do so, and fewer still in reality actually do so.

In an economic sense, we are all consumers, as to **consume** is to live life. Along with earning a living, present and future consumption are the most important means individuals employ for achieving their many unique ends in life. At any one point in time, ends are virtually infinite and means are finite and scarce. Thus the economic challenge arises, and hence the need for understanding economic laws and for these regulatory principles. Principles in accordance with such laws, over the flow of time, then allow for: greater freedom and property rights => greater entrepreneurship, specialization and innovation => greater savings, investment and capital => greater production, exchange and consumption ... at lesser costs and prices => and thus greater individual ends met with lesser means, or in other words, greater "pursuit of happiness".

Furthermore in regard to consumer **ends**, economist and physicist David Friedman states that: "Under any institutions, there are essentially only three ways that I can get another person to help me achieve my ends: love, trade, and force. ... By love I mean making my end your end. Those who love me wish me to get what I want. So they voluntarily, unselfishly, help me. ... The second method of cooperation is trade. I agree to help you achieve your end if you help me achieve mine. ... The third method is force. You do what I want or I shoot you." He then expands on love, which is very relevant to government intervention including regulation: "Love – more generally, the sharing of a common end – works well, but only for a limited range of problems. ... But for a complicated end involving a large number of people – producing [a] book, for instance – love will not work." In terms of many of the proponents of greater regulation: "The attack on private property ... implies that the alternative to selfish trade is unselfish love. But, under private property, love already functions where it can. Nobody is prevented from doing something for free if he wants to." Moreover: "There is no way to give a politician power that can be used only to do good. ... Political mechanisms, bureaus and bureaucrats, follow their own ends just as surely as individual entrepreneurs follow theirs." {Friedman 1989}

The father of David Friedman and fellow economist Milton Friedman famously asked in one of his books that later became a TV series, "[w]ho **protects** the consumer?" In doing this he firstly acknowledged that: "The market must, it is said, be supplemented by other arrangements in order to protect the consumer from himself and from avaricious sellers, and to protect all of us from the spillover neighborhood effects of market transactions." But: "The question is whether the arrangements that have been recommended or adopted to meet them, to supplement the market, are well devised for that purpose, or whether, as so often happens, the cure may not be worse than the disease." He highlighted a number of high profile regulatory cures that were worse for consumers than the so called market diseases: airplanes, automobiles, trains and trucks; consumer product safety; environmental pollution and resources; food and drugs; etc. This is because: "Government intervention in the marketplace is subject to laws of its own, not legislated laws, but scientific [economic] laws. It obeys forces and goes in directions that may have little relationship to the intentions or desires of its initiators or supporters." And: "It is present ... when government intervenes in the marketplace, whether to protect consumers against high prices or shoddy goods, to promote their safety, or to preserve the environment." So: "Ask yourself what products are currently least satisfactory and have shown the least improvement over time. ... The shoddy products are all produced by government or government-regulated industries. The outstanding products are all produced by private enterprise with little or no government involvement." He thus concluded that: "Perfection is not of this world. There will always be shoddy products, quacks, con artists. But on the whole, market competition, when it is permitted to work, protects the consumer better than do the alternative government mechanisms that have been increasingly superimposed on the market. ... [C]ompetition does not protect the consumer because businessmen are more soft-hearted than the bureaucrats or because they are more altruistic or generous, or even because they are more competent, but only because it is in the self-interest of the businessman to serve the consumer." {Friedman 1979}

From a PCT perspective, regulations largely **harm** consumers because as Eamonn Butler of the Adam Smith Institute summarised: "In [the political] struggle between interests, small groups with sharply focused interests have more influence in decision-making than much larger groups with more diffused concerns, such as consumers and taxpayers." Moreover: "[N]o voting system truly reflects the different strengths of opinion of all the individuals involved. Governments cannot possibly know the preferences of all their electors, so can hardly claim to know what is in the public interest." Thus: "The existence of market failure does not necessarily mean that government action is any better. ... Indeed, the problems that government intervention creates can be even more damaging than those it is intended to correct." And at an even deeper level: "[PCT] simply asks us to make the same assumptions about human behaviour in the political sphere as we make when we analyse markets." And therefore: "[I]f self-interest gives rise to certain outcomes in markets which some believe cause problems that politicians should try to fix, should we not assume that these same forces of self-interest exist within the political systems that try to 'correct' market failure? ... This self-interest operating in the political system will lead to government failure, which can be far more serious than market failure because of the coercive power that government exercises and because government is not subject to a direct competitive process." {Butler 2012}

From an ASE perspective, regulations largely harm consumers because, as economist Ludwig von Mises once said: "The essence of the interventionist policy [like regulation] is to take from one group to give to another. It is **confiscation** and distribution." This is economically unsustainable because: "First: Restrictive measures always restrict output and the amount of goods available for consumption. ... Second: All varieties of interference with the market phenomena not only fail to achieve the ends aimed at by their authors and supporters, but bring about a state of affairs which – from the point of view of their authors' and advocates' valuations – is less desirable than the previous state of affairs which they were designed to alter. ... Third: Interventionism aims at confiscating the surplus of one part of the population and at giving it to the other part. Once this surplus is exhausted by total confiscation, a further continuation of this policy is impossible." Despite all this, he warned that politically: "The failures of the interventionist policies [like regulation] do not in the least impair the popularity of the implied doctrine." {Mises 1949}

Regulations such as those pertaining to public infrastructure utilities and antitrust are great **examples** of ones purportedly initiated and maintained to protect consumers. The former was meant to directly protect consumers from so called natural monopolies. The latter was meant to indirectly protect consumers through protecting competition from monopolies, oligopolies and excessive market power. These were neither the true intentions nor, more importantly, the actual effects.

Regarding **antitrust**, Professor Dominick Armentano sums up the situation as follows: "[Over] more than a century of antitrust enforcement ... it is undeniably true that the antitrust laws have often been employed against innovative business organizations that have expanded output and lowered prices. That is most obvious in private antitrust cases (90% of all antitrust litigation), but it is also evident in the classic government cases as well." And: "Since antitrust regulation (at least the *Sherman Act*) was allegedly designed to prohibit business activity harmful to consumers' interests, much of antitrust policy as practiced, appears terribly misguided and might be termed a paradox." Yet: "If the laws were originally meant to protect less efficient business organizations from competition rather than to promote the interests of consumers, then there is no paradox ... [and thus] antitrust regulation is just another historical example of protectionist rent-seeking legislation." He also pointed out the "[f]aulty theorizing" at play, particularly in the 1950s and 1960s, regarding the understanding of competition and monopoly (and everything in-between) using industrial organization (IO) theory and the structure-conduct-performance (SCP) framework. {Armentano 1999} In particular, as economist Friedrich von Hayek once lectured: "[C]ompetition is by its nature a dynamic process whose essential characteristics are assumed away by the assumptions underlying static analysis [thus] perfect competition means indeed the absence of all competitive activities." {Hayek 1968} Although Austrian economists have always challenged this static IO theory and mechanical SCP framework, mainstream economists also began to challenge this in the 1970s and 1980s leading to changes in the nature and lessening in the amount of antitrust enforcement. Unfortunately, there has been a new wave of antitrust activism since the 1990s. {Armentano 1999}

The little known history of public **infrastructure** utilities such as electricity and gas, in the USA at least, teaches that there was plenty of effective competition prior to the less effective competitors lobbying for market protection regulation in exchange for economic oversight regulation. In fact, the regulation of such so called natural monopolies started decades before the theory and main economic justification was created. Such regulation first started federally with rail in the 1870s, and at state level with utilities from 1907 in Wisconsin. {DiLorenzo 1996} The most modern forms of utility regulation were much later adopted in the UK from the 1980s, and Australia and elsewhere from the 1990s. The economic paradox is, even if a public utility monopoly were indeed natural – ie could produce at a lower total cost than all others, actual and potential – it would still not be in need of all of the other types of regulations, intentionally or unintentionally, preventing entry and rivalry in these markets and even those upstream and downstream as well.

References:

- David Friedman, *Machinery of Freedom: Guide to a Radical Capitalism*, 1989

- Dominick Armentano, *Antitrust: The Case for Repeal*, 1999

- Eamonn Butler, *Public Choice: A Primer*, 2012

- Friedrich von Hayek, *Competition as a Discovery Procedure*, 1968

- Ludwig von Mises, *Human Action: A Treatise on Economics*, 1949

- Milton & Rose Friedman, *Free To Choose: A Personal Statement*, 1979

- Thomas DiLorenzo, *The Myth of Natural Monopoly*, 1996

5. Regulations kill

Certain regulations can unintentionally but predictably kill people in the shorter term, and the list of these regulations grows over time as all regulations grow.

Regulations are of course never intended, publicly or privately, to kill or physically harm people. Not at least in Australia and other modern capitalistic democracies. This is putting to one side, for the moment, the small but growing radical environmentalists who wish to de-populate the planet and have us return to a hunter-gatherer society or at least to a modified dark ages with them continuing to live in relative comfort as the ruling elite. Regulations, such as those related to drugs, health and guns, can **unintentionally** but predicably kill or harm by omission in the short term. Regulations, such as those related to energy, chemicals and the environment, can unintentionally but predicably kill or harm by omission in the medium term. Just having way too many regulations overall of any sort can unintentionally but predicably kill or harm by omission in the long term through less economic efficiency, growth and jobs. A number of the plethora of current and historical examples of killer and harmful regulations are provided next. But note that there are many additional examples of alleged killer and harmful products that are and were not so, yet were regulated to 'death' anyway. These are not covered in this publication. (see Contoski 1997 and DiLorenzo 2004 for more)

One of the oldest and most common forms of regulation that can ultimately kill and harm, and did so relatively quickly in pre-industrial times, is **price-control** and rationing. As economist and historian Thomas DiLorenzo says: "The case against price controls

– no matter how they are labeled by politicians – has been well known for hundreds of years. By artificially stimulating demand while taking some or all of the profitability out of supply, price controls inevitably create shortages. They also induce suppliers to skimp on quality, to the extent that they can, and often lead to bizarre government-imposed rationing schemes that only make things worse." Far more importantly: "The case against price controls is not merely an academic exercise, however, restricted to economics textbooks. There is a four thousand year historical record of economic catastrophe after catastrophe caused by price controls." (see Scheuttinger & Butler 1978 for more) Professor DiLorenzo cites many of these historical examples of death and harm including: "In 284 A.D. the Roman emperor Diocletian created inflation by placing too much money in circulation, and then fixed the maximum prices at which beef, grain, eggs, clothing and other articles could be sold, and prescribed the penalty of death for anyone who disposed of his wares at a higher figure. The results were that 'the people brought provisions no more to markets, since they could not get a reasonable price for them and this increased the dearth so much, that at last after many had died by it, the law itself was set aside'." And: "French politicians repeated the same mistakes after their revolution, putting into place the 'Law of the Maximum' in 1793, which first imposed price controls on grain, and then on a long list of other items. Predictably, in some French towns, the people were so badly fed that they were collapsing in the streets from lack of nourishment. The French government was forced to abolish its disastrous price control law after it had literally killed thousands." {DiLorenzo 2012}

One of the more current and ongoing examples of killer regulation is that under the US Food and Drug Administration (FDA). "[F]ederal regulations on **pharmaceuticals** are intended to protect the public by ensuring that the drugs sold are not just safe but also effective for their particular uses. However, this intervention causes new drugs, ultimately shown to be safe and effective, to be introduced in the market years later than they otherwise would have been. As a result, many people die or suffer unnecessarily." This is according to Susan Dudley and Jerry Brito of the Mercatus Center. {Dudley & Brito 2012} Economist Milton Friedman added that: "Of course it is desirable that the public be protected from unsafe and useless drugs. However, it is also desirable that new drug development should be stimulated, and that new drugs should be made available to those who can benefit from them as soon as possible. As is so often the case, one good objective conflicts with other good objectives. Safety and caution in one direction can mean death in another." {Friedman 1979} His economist son, David Friedman, is even more forthright when he proclaims: "Caution kills. Whom it kills may not be obvious; often the new drug is only an improvement on an old one, an improvement which might raise a cure rate from 80% to 85%. Which men and women and children make up the 5% killed by caution no one can ever know; their deaths are statistics, not headlines. A statistical corpse is just as real as a thalidomide baby on the front page; it is just less visible. Visibility is an important element in politics and the FDA is a political institution. Given a choice between one tragedy on the front page and ten in the medical statistics, it inevitably prefers the latter. It thus has a strong bias in favor of overregulating, of stifling medical progress in the name of caution." {Friedman 1989}

A less obvious example comes from the field of energy. As pointed out by Heartland president Joe Bast: "Increasing Corporate Average Fuel Economy (CAFE) **standards** have a terrible unintended consequence: needless highway deaths. … CAFE standards caused between 1,300 and 2,600 traffic deaths every year since they were established in 1975. This is because the best way to achieve fuel economy is to build lighter cars, which do not protect passengers as well as heavier vehicles during traffic accidents." {Bast 2008} In addition, even if so called capitalist-caused climate change (or global warming, cooling or weirding) were real and proved, which Heartland and many others have shown that they are not, higher prices and lower reliability of electricity and gas can kill and harm the most vulnerable through insufficient cooling in summer heat waves and insufficient heating in winter cold spells. A number of regulations drive this, chief amongst these are a century of slowly growing public utility regulation and decades of vastly growing environmental regulations spearheaded by the US Environmental Protection Agency (EPA) and its increasingly minionised state-based government agencies.

Milton Friedman talked more about **environmental** regulations and the driving force behind these of environmentalism: "Public discussion of the environmental issue is frequently characterized more by emotion than reason. Much of it proceeds as if the issue is pollution versus no pollution, as if it were desirable and possible to have a world without pollution." But: "That is clearly nonsense. No one who contemplates the problem seriously will regard zero pollution as either a desirable or a possible state of affairs." This is because: "We could have zero pollution from automobiles, for example, by simply abolishing all automobiles. That would also make the kind of agricultural and industrial productivity we now enjoy impossible, and so condemn most of us to a drastically lower standard of living, perhaps many even to death." {Friedman 1979}

Regarding **health**, Heartland's Steve Karnick weighes in on regulatory death and harm as follows: "Inherent in single-payer health care plans is allowing a relatively small number of elected officials and unelected bureaucrats to make life-and-death decisions affecting others, substituting their judgment for the voluntary and better-informed choices of millions of patients and their doctors." And hence: "When government agencies replace markets, those with the most political clout are rewarded with the best and most timely treatment. Everyone else must wait in lines for treatment and are more likely to die from denial of services." {Karnick 2007}

Mark Thornton is one of many economists to have examined **prohibition** related regulations and its all-too-frequent consequences of greater crime and crime related deaths and harm: "[S]tudies have shown an association between the consumption of certain drugs, such as alcohol and heroin, and criminal behavior. This relationship was a crucial reason for the implementation of several prohibitions, including of alcohol, cocaine, and marijuana. Another motive for enacting prohibition legislation is to reduce corruption of both public officials and the democratic process." But: "In general, prohibition results in more, not less, crime and corruption. The black markets that result from prohibitions represent institutionalized criminal exchanges. These criminal exchanges, or victimless crimes, often involve violent criminal acts. Prohibitions have also been associated with organized crime and gangs. Violence is used in black markets and criminal organizations to enforce contracts, maintain market share, and defend sales territory." Thus: "The crime and violence that occurred during the late 1920s and early 1930s was a major reason for the repeal of [alcohol] Prohibition." {Thornton 1991} Crime and crime related deaths are even higher due to unconstitutional gun regulation that mainly restricts non-criminal gun usage, as "[d]eterrence matters not only to those who actively take defensive actions." {Lott 2010}

References:

- David Friedman, *Machinery of Freedom: Guide to a Radical Capitalism*, 1989
- Edmund Contoski, *Makers and Takers: How Wealth and Progress Are Made and How They Are Taken Away or Prevented*, 1997
- Joe Bast, *Ten Principles of Energy Policy*, 2008
- John Lott, *More Guns, Less Crime: Understanding Crime and Gun Control Laws*, 2010
- Mark Thornton, *The Economics of Prohibition*, 1991
- Milton & Rose Friedman, *Free To Choose: A Personal Statement*, 1979
- Robert Scheuttinger & Eamonn Butler, *Forty Centuries of Wage and Price Controls: How Not to Fight Inflation*, 1978
- Steve Karnick, *Ten Principles of Health Care Policy*, 2007
- Susan Dudley & Jerry Brito, *Regulation: A Primer*, 2012
- Thomas DiLorenzo, *Organized Crime: The Unvarnished Truth About Government*, 2012

6. Cost benefit analysis can improve regulation

In conjunction with comparative risk assessment, cost benefit analysis should be used (early and often) by legislators and regulation-makers in assessing the need for and nature of any new regulation plus the reform and removal of existing ones.

Cost benefit analysis (CBA) is a practical microeconomics method and **frame-of-mind** for better informing government policy (eg economic, social and environmental) and investment (eg financial, budgetary and regulatory) decisions regarding net benefits or costs (NBC). The key to CBA is identifying and quantifying all of the relevant impacts of a given policy or investment (versus other scarce choices) as both benefits and costs, from one or more viewpoints, in terms of money, and discounted for time.

CBA most explicitly recognises that human wants or ends are infinite and (human and non-human) resources or means are finite and, thus, **decisions** have to be made between alternative human actions (eg projects) that compete for resources (eg time, effort, etc). There are always alternative government policies or investments so there are always decisions to be made … even if the choice is to do nothing. This is the essence of resource allocation efficiency – ie that scarce resources go to their most highly valued uses over time.

CBA attempts to value all benefits and costs in terms of **money** (be it inflation adjusted or not), even those things that are not already valued as such. Money is considered the best *numeraire* to use in CBA (and many other circumstances) because it is the only objective measure of value (or more technically correct, price) that allows convenient comparisons between benefits and costs of vastly different situations and actions, many of which have already been valued in private markets or in government budgets.

Government-related CBAs are usually undertaken from a social **viewpoint** (ie standing) such as that of a disadvantaged group of persons, a region or a government – ie a social and/or external CBA. However, CBA is more often done outside of government from a business entity's viewpoint but goes under the name of profitability, investment or asset value analysis – ie a private CBA. CBA can be used after (ie *ex post* CBA), before (ie *ex ante* CBA) or during (ie *in medias res* CBA) a situation or action (eg project, program or policy). All three CBAs (above) can be used within one situation or action (eg with no counter-factual), or across a number of situations or actions (eg with one or more counter-factuals).

To make benefits and costs comparable over **time** (especially over two or more years) requires discounting at some rate. The discount rate can determine the acceptance or rejection of a given alternative and alter the ranking of two or more alternatives. The need for discounting reflects the general preference for the present over the future and the opportunity cost to invest for a return – ie the time value of money.

The following could be considered inputs to, complements of, substitutes for or otherwise **alternatives** to a partial or full CBA:

- computable general equilibrium models (CGEM), input-output models (IOM) & multiplier analysis (MPA);

- cost effectiveness analysis (CEA) & cost utility analysis (CUA);

- environmental impact analysis (EIA), regulatory impact analysis (RIA) & social impact analysis (SIA).

None of these alternatives is as complete, economically sound or universally applicable as CBA. Only CEA or CUA comes close, and are best used when a full quantitative CBA is not practical.

The full quantitative CBA **processes** typically include the following types of steps and activities:

- 1) defining & deciding:

    o   a) the goals of the situation or action (X) of concern (eg. outputs/outcomes sought from policy or investment project);

    o   b) on none, one or more 'counter-factual' alternatives (Y) to the policy or investment project;

    o   c) from who's viewpoint/s will benefits and costs be analysed (ie standing);

    o   d) on one or more CBA 'success' decision criteria such as net present value (NPV), benefit cost ratio (BCR), internal rate of return (IRR), net benefit investment ratio (NBIR) &/or social return on investment (SROI);

- 2) identifying & quantifying:

    o   e) non-money impacts or quantities (Q) of the policy or investment project (eg outputs/outcomes achieved);

    o   f) money values or prices ($P) of the benefits & costs (eg social = external + private);

    o   g) risk & uncertainty (R&U) … directly into impacts or values, or indirectly into the discount rate;

    o   h) inflation (I) … directly into values, or indirectly into the discount rate;

- 3) calculating & comparing:

    o   i) aggregate benefits ($B) less aggregate costs ($C) – ie net benefits or costs ($NBC = $B - $C);

    o   j) discounted net benefits or costs ($DNBC), at one or more discount rates (DR%);

o   k) decision criteria (DC) such as NPV of project X > $0 &/or NPV of project X > NPV of project Y;

o   l) distributions of $B, $C & $DNBC (eg at least, those with CBA standing);

o   m) sensitivities of DR and I, as well as the key Ps, Qs & R&Us (eg at least, best-case, worst-case & most-likely-case).

Two key CBA steps (from above) where outcomes meet CBA **values** are: 2e) the identification and quantification of non-money outcomes (Q), known as impacts analysis; and 2f) the identification and quantification of money benefits ($B) and money costs ($C), known as values or pricing analysis ($P). Values or prices are either market or shadow. Market prices are observed. Shadow prices are derived using stated or revealed preference methods, or (more typically) from existing plug-in studies of these methods.

$$\$B = \$P^{\text{B}}_{\text{value}} \times Q^{\text{B}}_{\text{impact}}$$
$$\$C = \$P^{\text{C}}_{\text{value}} \times Q^{\text{C}}_{\text{impact}}$$

Three other key CBA steps (from above) where values meet **time** are: 3i) separately summing all of the benefits ($B) and costs ($C), and then subtracting the latter from the former ($NBC = $B - $C); 3j) discounting net benefits or costs ($DNBC or NBC_{\text{time}}$), at one or more discount rates (DR%); and 3k) making use of one or more decision criteria (DC). Discounting is akin to the inverse of compounding on a bank savings account and thus DR as the inverse of an interest rate.

$$\$NBC_{\text{time}} = \Sigma\,[\,\$B\,/\,(1+DR)_{\text{time}}] - \Sigma\,[\,\$C\,/\,(1+DR)_{\text{time}}] = \Sigma\,[\,\$NBC\,/\,(1+DR)_{\text{time}}\,]$$

CBA **recommendations** should centre around one or more of the following DC:

• $NPV = NPV($NBC) = PV($B) / PV($C):

o   accept if $NPV ≥ $0 or $NPV(X) > $NPV(Y) then choose X;

o   reject if $NPV < $0 or if $NPV(Y) > $NPV(X) then choose Y;

- BCR% = PV($B) / PV($C):

  ○ accept if BCR% ≥ 1 where $NPV ≥ $0;

  ○ reject if BCR% < 1 where $NPV < $0;

- IRR% = IRR(DR%) = PV($B) = PV($C) = NPV = $0:

  ○ accept if IRR% ≥ DR%;

  ○ reject if IRR% < DR%;

- NBIR% = [NPV($NBC) – PV($OpEx)] / [PV($CapEx)];

- SROI% = [NPV($NBC)] / [PV($OpEx) + PV($CapEx)]. {Nelson 2015}

One of the most famous and serious attempted **applications** of a proper CBA system came in February 1981 as a result of *Executive Order 12291* by President Ronald Reagan. Amongst other things, it aimed to: reduce the burdens of existing and future regulations; increase agency accountability for regulatory actions; provide for presidential oversight of the regulatory process; minimize duplication and conflict of regulations; and insure well-reasoned regulations. The process included regulatory agencies submitting proposed major regulations to the Office of Information and Regulatory Affairs (OIRA); proposed regulations being subjected to CBA by OIRA; and then regulations being promulgated by an agency, even those rejected by OIRA. Perhaps not surprisingly given this last point, there were mixed results under this Order. More fundamentally, the: "Reagan campaign against regulation failed to attract public support, in part because the regulatory reforms appear no more legitimate than the regulations themselves" and thus "fail[ed] to orchestrate systematic change". {Cowen 1998} In Australia, the federal Office of Best Practice Regulation (OBPR) uses a combination of CBA, regulatory impact statements (RIS), and business cost calculator (BCC). A RIS is a document prepared by the one responsible for a regulatory proposal, following consultation with stakeholders. It formalises and provides evidence of the key steps taken during the development of the proposal, and includes CBA. The BCC is an IT-based tool designed to assist in estimating the business compliance costs of various options. It provides an automated and standard process for quantifying compliance costs of regulation on business using an activity based costing (ABC) methodology. The BCC can be accessed by anyone in the world for free. {OBPR websire} The BCC in part helped to inspire and inform the Mercatus Center's regulatory cost calculator (RCC) in the USA, which can also be accessed by anyone in the world for free. {Mercatus website}

Unsurprisingly and not unreasonably, there are a number of important **criticisms** of CBA. Some criticisms for example suggest that CBA is impractical because: "[T]he problems of regulation stem from the poor incentives and information of regulators. Simply doing a cost-benefit study, and telling regulators to think about or weigh the results, is unlikely to improve policy outcomes or strike down bad regulations." Thus: "When attempting to construct a program of regulatory reform ... [CBA] should not take the primary seat." However: "Within the practical realm of regulatory reform, [CBA] must take on the status of a veto mechanism, if it is to have any bite at all. That is, agencies must somehow be influenced or constrained to reject policies that fail a cost-benefit test." {Cowen 1998} Other criticisms for instance suggest that CBA is conceptually invalid as: "Costs are subjective and therefore social costs and social value, as the terms are typically construed, do not exist as either measurable or even theoretical concepts." And yet: "The standard approach is dependent upon being able to measure and therefore make objective these concepts." Therefore: "This inherently involves making interpersonal utility comparisons and the summing of interpersonal evaluations across individuals. Neither of these can be held as methodologically valid." {Cordato 2007}

Conducting CBA on the impacts of regulation and on different alternatives to regulation is complicated and difficult to do successfully, but adds critical **information** to the debate. In particular, CBA is likely to at least help legislators and regulation-makers to better understand that there are always 'two sides to a coin' – ie there are both benefits and costs to every situation and activity, which will accrue to someone over time. CBA, in itself, cannot make decisions however. Decisions still have to be made according to judgement not just analysis. CBA should, nevertheless, help make more rigorous and objective information available to regulation and reform processes.

References:

- Darren Brady Nelson, *Introduction to Cost Benefit Analysis*, 2015

- Mercatus Center, https://mercatus.org/publication/regulatory-cost-calculator, 2017

- Office of Best Practice Regulation, https://bcc.obpr.gov.au/, 2017

- Roy Cordato, *Toward an Austrian Theory of Environmental Economics*, 2007

- Tyler Cowen, *Using Cost-Benefit Analysis to Review Regulation*, 1998

7. Comparative risk assessment can improve regulation

In conjunction with (or as a substitute for) cost benefit analysis, comparative risk assessment can also be used by legislators and regulation-makers in assessing the need for and nature of any new regulation plus the reform of existing ones.

There are many **definitions** of comparative risk assessment (CRA), most coming from the literature on risks to the environment as well as human health and safety. One such definition is: "[A] systematic process to estimate the level of risk related to some specific action or activity. It is now commonly applied to a wide variety of human endeavours in which harm to people, the environment or economic interests might occur." {WHO 2012} Another one is: "[T]he comparison of different environmental problems to determine their relative risk to human health and quality of life, as well as risks to the natural environment. These comparisons typically take the shape of a ranked list with some issues identified as posing higher risks than others." {Jones 1997}

Risk itself, and the related concept of uncertainty, were in particular pioneered by Frank Knight. He defined risk as follows: "Risk refers to situations in which the outcome of an event is unknown, but the decision-maker knows the range of possible outcomes and the probabilities of each, such that anyone with the same information and beliefs would make the same prediction." He then added that: "**Uncertainty**, by contrast, characterizes situations in which the range of possible outcomes, let alone the relevant probabilities, is unknown. In this case the decision maker cannot follow a formal decision rule but must rely on an intuitive understanding of the situation – 'judgment' – to anticipate what may occur." And summarized the two inter-related concepts thusly: "Risk, in this sense, refers to a quantity susceptible of measurement, and not a true uncertainty that cannot be quantified." {Klein 2010} Economist Ludwig von Mises further explained risk versus uncertainty when he: "[D]istinguished between class probability and case probability. The former describes situations in which an event may be classified as a unique element of a homogeneous class, the properties of which are known. Case probability applies to cases in which each event is unique, such that no general class probabilities can be defined." {Klein 2010} This built upon his brother Richard von Mises's defence of: "[F]requentism, the idea that … probabilities can be defined only in cases in which repeated trials are feasible – ie in situations where each event can be meaningfully compared to other events in the same class … [and] probabilities can only be defined *ex post*, as learned through experience, and cannot exist *a priori*." Hence, Ludwig von Mises went a bit further than Knight when he succinctly called uncertainty: "[A]s a case in which probabilities, in the frequentist sense, do not exist." {Klein 2010}

The most popularly known risk-related concept is the so called **precautionary** principle championed by the modern environmental movement. It is essentially about taking so called protective action, without undue delay, before there is complete or sufficient scientific information or proof of a risk. This in effect inappropriately reverses the burden-of-proof from such typical plaintiffs as government, environmentalists and alarmists to the typical defendants such as businesses, consumers and sceptics. Another further criticism of this principle is it: "[D]emands that the initiator of an activity proves its complete harmlessness and that the government does not need to prove probable harm in order to stop it. Proving that something is absolutely innocuous is impracticable in new domains, where learning is performed by trial-and-error, and therefore this principle would paralyze innovation." Because: "Knowledge acquisition is costly, and full knowledge is impossible." {Capella 2009} Even worse still: "[I]t prevents scientific debate. This is what makes the principle so dangerous." Which generates: "[A] quasi-religious bigotry which history should have has taught us to fear." {SIRC Undated}

In the spirit of the precautionary principle, the Harvard Center for Risk Analysis stated that: "The role of federal regulatory agencies in protecting citizens from risks to human health safety, and the environment has increased dramatically in the last [four score or more] ... [as] they pursue their mandates to make life safer and healthier for citizens and, in the case of environmental **regulation**, for plant and animal species." {Harvard 1995} Depending on whose viewpoint, there are risks and uncertainty to reforming the current stock and future flow of such regulation. And: "There are ... substantial benefits from federal risk regulation. For example, the United States has made substantial progress in cleaning up air, water and land, in part due to the strong regulatory presence of federal government." Thus, Harvard claim: "[C]omplete elimination of risk regulation is not a desirable course and has few serious advocates." But they conceded that: "[R]isk regulation can be made more effective and less costly without becoming less democratic or less equitable." {Harvard 1995}

On the other hand, again depending on who's viewpoint, there are also risks and uncertainty to not **reforming** such regulation, because as Joe Bast of Heartland pointed out: "Regulations impose heavy burdens on businesses and individuals, yet frequently produce few if any social benefits." For example: "An analysis of the relation between federal regulation – measured by the number of pages in the Federal Register – and output per unit of capital, economic growth, and productivity showed that every 1% point increase of the ratio of regulation to capital correlates with a 0.24% point decrease in capital productivity." {Bast 2010} The Bast viewpoint arguably represents a much larger population of consumers, businesses and voters than that of Harvard.

Dr Robert Higgs of the Independent Institute poses the following **logic** challenge to those wanting Bigger Government: "[W]e might well apply the precautionary principle ... to the state's establishment and operation [of ever larger and growing regulation], the state's supporters would appear to stagger under a burden of proof they cannot support with either logic or evidence. Yet, almost incomprehensibly, [these] people fear that without [this] supposedly all-important [over regulation], society will lapse into disorder and people will suffer grave harm." {Higgs 2007}

One typical approach to **CRA** is as follows: "The first step ... is the development of a conceptual model or framework that combines knowledge of risk-affecting factors and how they could interact to cause harm. In many cases this information can be expressed mathematically as a series of equations that, provided sufficient quantitative data and knowledge exist, enable quantification of the risk or, at least, the relative risk." In addition: "The risk assessment task is often broken down into four discrete components: Hazard Identification – which involves describing the hazard; Hazard Characterization – which presents information about characteristics; and Exposure Assessment – which attempts to estimate the exposure of the affected population(s)." {WHO 2012}

It is important to note that risk can and is also addressed within **CBA** itself. The main approaches are: discount rate; sensitivity analysis; expected value; option price; and option value. The first two approaches are the most common. However, the second three approaches are the better ones.

References:

- Francisco Capella, *The Ethics of Freedom and Climate Change*, 2009

- Harvard Center for Risk Analysis, *Reform of Risk Regulation: More Protection at Less Cost*, 1995

- Joe Bast, *Ten Principles for Improved Business Climates*, 2010

- Ken Jones, *Retrospective On Ten Years of Comparative Risk*, 1997

- Peter Klein, *The Capitalist and the Entrepreneur: Essays on Organizations and Markets*, 2010

- Robert Higgs, *If Men Were Angels: The Basic Analytics of the State versus Self-government*, 2007

- Social Issues Research Centre, *Beware the Precautionary Principle*, Undated

- World Health Organization, *Comparative Risk Analysis*, 2012

8. Repeal existing regulations before adopting new ones

Repealing should be legislators and regulation-makers 'first best' tool for slowing down the flow, stopping the flow and then reversing the flow and reducing the stock of regulations.

To **repeal** a regulation is: "To revoke or rescind, especially by an official or formal act." {Black's website} Repealing should be legislators and regulation-makers first best tool for slowing down the flow, stopping the flow, and then reversing the flow as well as reducing the stock of regulations. Once a regulation is on the books, it is very difficult to reform through further changes in favour of free and competitive markets, and thus to the net benefit of most consumers, businesses and voters. It is even more difficult to repeal.

History thus far has been largely on the side of not repealing regulations, and even at times repealing regulations and then later restoring them. One inspiring exception to this general trend was the British repeal of the anti-free-trade Corn Laws in the mid 1800s, which had for decades established an enormous import tariff on wheat. In fact, the UK Parliament went on to repeal more laws in that era than were passed. {Friedman 1979} Classical liberal Herbert Spencer documented the following: "[F]rom the Statute of Merton [in 1236] to the end of 1872, there had been passed 18,110 public Acts; of which [an] estimated four-fifths had been wholly or partially repealed. [A]lso the number of public Acts repealed wholly or in part, or amended, during the three years 1870-71-72 had been 3,532, of which 2,759 had been totally repealed." {Spencer 1851} Some inspiring repeal episodes in US history include: President Thomas Jefferson at the start of the

1800s re some tax, tariff and other laws; President Andrew Jackson in the early 1800s re central banking; President Martin van Buren in mid 1800s re financial laws; President Andrew Johnson in mid-to-late 1800s re Southern military occupation and reconstruction; and President Ronald Reagan in the 1980s re central banking and antitrust. Honourable deregulation mentions are also deserved for Presidents Washington, Grant and Truman, but surprisingly not so much for Harding and Coolidge when it came to deregulation as opposed to taxation and other areas. {Denson 2001}

"Once passed, regulations are often difficult to **change** or repeal. Markets, on the other hand, can change quickly." This is according to Heartland president Joe Bast, who also highlights one of the main reasons for this as follows: "Regulations are difficult to update and repeal because interest groups hire staff with expertise in the most arcane details of the laws, and often with personal relationships with elected officials who serve on oversight committees. Having invested time and resources in shaping and complying with existing regulations, these groups often line up to oppose change." He also makes the following crucial point for this century in particular: "All regulations eventually become obsolete, perhaps starting the day a bill becomes law. Technological change, which is most visible in telecommunications but is occurring in every part of the economy, makes regulatory obsolescence a bigger problem than ever before." This is due to: "Obsolete regulations impos[ing] unnecessary costs on businesses and consumers by discouraging innovation and rewarding investment in compliance and lobbying activities that produce little consumer value." He concludes that: "The lesson from telecommunications regulation is that one of the great but often unnoticed benefits of deregulation is not having to constantly revise and reform existing regulations. Markets are able to make millions of adjustments to the expressed interests of millions of consumers in a single day, while regulatory reform is invariably slow and confrontational." {Bast 2010}

There are many **approaches** to repeal. Ideally it is either a flat-out repeal of a stock of existing regulations identified as problem ones and/or a mechanism over time for keeping the flow of new regulations under control through in-and-out rules like one-for-one, one-for-two, etc. One of the most widely known in-and-out rule is that of the Stossel Rule by libertarian media pundit John Stossel. In his own words: "It's simple: For every new regulation bureaucrats pass, they must repeal five old ones." {FoxNews website} However, when it comes to repeal, the burden-of-proof should be on those wanting to keep a regulation not the other way around. This burden should furthermore be high like that of beyond-a-reasonable-doubt in criminal law rather than moderate like that of on-the-balance-of-probabilities in civil law. CBA and CRA (discussed above) should be able to assist for better understanding by both sides of the argument of repeal versus keep … and, if the latter, keep as-is versus keep but change.

The supporting logic for this was arguably best put forward by economist, philosopher, historian and jurisprudence scholar Murray Rothbard who reasoned: "When people are free to act, they will always act in a way that they believe will maximize their **utility**. … Any exchange that takes place on the free market occurs because of the expected benefit to each party concerned. If we allow ourselves to use the term society to depict the pattern of all individual exchanges, then we may say that the free market maximizes social utility, since everyone gains in utility." Hence he further reasoned that: "Coercive [regulation], on the other hand, signifies *per se* that the individual or individuals coerced would not have done what they are now doing were it not for the [regulation]. … The coerced individual loses in utility as a result of the [regulation], for his action has been changed by its impact. … [I]n [regulation], at least one, and sometimes both, of the pair of would-be exchangers lose in utility." {Rothbard 1977}

The Johnston Test is a good example of a tangible repeal methodology for "asking whether current and proposed regulations are justified, and repealing those that flunk the test". Bast thus argues that "simply by" doing this that "society could benefit to the tune of hundreds of billions of dollars a year". In essence, this **test**: "[A]sks whether the original conditions that may have called for regulation still exist and whether there are other ways to accomplish the same objective without relying on regulation." More specifically: "[I]ndustries are most often regulated when three conditions are present: the product or service is subject to substantial shifts in supply and demand; supply reliability cannot be achieved through precautionary stocks or other market techniques; and substantial social costs are incurred when supplies are interrupted." Therefore: "The intended effect of regulation in such cases is to improve the stability of supply by encouraging extra investment in reliability." In addition and in conclusion: "Even better, the test seems simple and intuitive enough that it can be put to work immediately, by elected officials and non-specialists." {Bast 2010}

Modern classical liberal George Reisman's suggestion of establishing a "Deregulation Agency" is a good example of a tangible repeal **institution**. "Its powers would supersede those of any regulatory agency. ... [I]ts powers would be limited to the repeal of existing regulations, including the narrowing of their scope in conditions in which considerations of political expediency prevented their total repeal. ... Ideally, the agency would possess the power to render any or all of them null and void." And, also: "As a minimum, the enabling legislation for the agency should require it, within a fairly short period of time, such as three years, to reduce the cost of government interference in the economic system as a whole by a minimum of 50%. Further reductions of at least 2% per year would be achieved thereafter." {Reisman 1998}

The **list** of potential regulations for partial or full repeal is unbelievably large, but should include those in the areas of: automobiles and manufacturing; aviation and airports; banking and finance; certain professions and other services; communication and entertainment; energy and environment; health and safety; land and planning; public utilities; rail and roads; and school and college education. Regardless of which particular regulations are examined and reformed first, legislators and policy-makers must never horse-trade to the point of taking two steps back to go one step forward towards free and competitive markets. {Rothbard 1982}

References

- Black's Law Dictionary, http://thelawdictionary.org/, 2017

- Fox News, http://www.foxnews.com/, 2017

- George Reisman, *Capitalism: A Treatise on Economics*, 1998

- Herbert Spencer, *The Man versus The State*, 1851

- Joe Bast, *Why Regulate? New Applications of the Johnston Test*, 2010

- John Denson, *Reassessing the Presidency The Rise of the Executive State and the Decline of Freedom*, 2001

- Milton & Rose Friedman, *Free To Choose: A Personal Statement*, 1979

- Murray Rothbard, *Power and Market: Government and the Economy*, 1977

- Murray Rothbard, *The Ethics of Liberty*, 1982

9. Enforcing property rights can be superior to regulation

Economics and history show that the greater use of property rights can usually better address areas of apparent market failure than regulation can, without the accompanying government failure and other unintended negative consequences.

Along with crime, tort and contract, property is the oldest area of common **law**, particularly that of real or land property. Common law was historically not government legislation or regulation driven law. One legal definition of property is: "The ownership of a thing is the right of one or more persons to possess and use it to the exclusion of others." Another legal definition of property rights is: "The rights given to the person or persons who have a right to own the property through purchase or bequest." And it is importantly noted that: "These are basic rights in any society though absolute right for a property is rare in any society." {Black's website}

Along with liberty and prices, private property **rights** are the most important for the functioning of free and competitive markets. Yet despite this, "one of the most misunderstood concepts is a strong system of property rights" {Alchian 2008} and by-and-large "free-market economists [have] paid little attention to the entities actually being exchanged on the very market they have advocated so strongly" {Rothbard 1973} – i.e. the exchange of ownership titles, usually money in exchange for goods or services. In economics, a property right is often thought of as: "[T]he exclusive authority to determine how a resource is used, whether that resource is owned by government or by individuals." This was economist Armen Alchian's take. He further described the key attributes of a private property right as follows: "(1) exclusivity of rights to choose the use of a resource; (2) exclusivity of rights to the services of a resource; and (3) rights to exchange the resource at mutually agreeable terms." {Alchian 2008} In discussing property rights and justice, economist Murray Rothbard quoted philosopher John Lock who famously said long ago that firstly: "[E]very man has a property in his own person." Secondly: "Whatsoever, then, he removes out of the state that nature hath provided and left it in, he hath mixed his labour with it, and joined to it something that is his own, and thereby makes it his property." And thus property: "[E]xcludes the common right of other men." {Rothbard 1973}

There has been a debate though much of modern history on whether **government** is needed or not for "a strong system of property rights", and if the former is answered in the affirmative then the debate switches to the exact nature of this (and to what degree) – eg relying more on the legislative and executive branches versus more on the judicial. Most, such as economist Adam Smith, said largely yes to such a need for government: "According to the system of natural liberty, the sovereign has only three duties to attend to" and the second of these include the establishment, definition and enforcement of property rights or in his own words "the duty of protecting, as far as possible, every member of the society from the injustice or oppression of every other member of it, or the duty of establishing an exact administration of justice". {Smith 1776} But others, such as politically economy writer Claude Frédéric Bastiat, said largely no to such a need for government: "Life, liberty, and property do not exist because men have made laws. On the contrary, it was the fact that life, liberty, and property existed beforehand that caused men to make [common] laws in the first place." {Bastiat 1853}

It is all too easy for interventions like regulation to **harm** the system of property rights, even one that the same government itself largely governs. This is why economist Friedrich von Hayek warned that: "Even if such power is not in itself bad, its exercise is likely to impede the functioning of those spontaneous ordering forces by which, without understanding them, man is in fact so largely assisted in the pursuit of his aims." {Hayek 1974} And when it comes to regulation more specifically, or as Rothbard called it "triangular intervention" with "a pair of exchangers or would-be exchangers", he stated that in such circumstances "at least one, and sometimes both, of the pair of would-be exchangers lose in utility" from such regulation which "compels a pair of people to make an exchange or prohibits them from doing so". For the purposes of analysis, he divided triangular intervention into two types: "price control, which deals with the terms of an exchange, and product control, which deals with the nature of the product or of the producer." He also warned that: "In tracing the effects of intervention, one must take care to analyze all its consequences, direct and indirect ... of every one of the almost infinite number of possible varieties of intervention." {Rothbard 1977}

So called market failure is nowadays the most common economic **rationale**, *ex ante* and/or *ex post*, for regulation in the first place. The main types of market failure are: 1) imperfect competition; 2) imperfect information; and 3) the existence of externalities including public goods. Some relevant types of regulations to these include: 1) antitrust and public utilities; 2) financial and health; and 3) environmental and safety. Regulation has all too often been evaluated in terms of ideal or perfect government versus imperfect or failed markets. Furthermore, many would argue that regulation often creates some or many of the market failures in the first place, whether unintentional or not. Given this, better use of property rights is the first-best solution over more second-best regulation and possible government failure.

Nobel laureate Ronald Coase helped to put property rights back in the economic policy spotlight, particularly in the context of **externalities**, using what became to be known as the Coase Theorem by his fellow economist George Stigler. Coase applied his original transaction costs approach, that he developed decades before in analysing business firms, to the problem of social costs. This theorem in essence asserts that where property is well defined, markets are competitive and transaction costs are minimal or zero then externalities can be bargained away by the concerned parties themselves. When this is not the case then an unconcerned third party like regulators or the courts can allocate social costs to one or the other parties or in between to the net benefit of society. As Coase said: "Nothing could be more anti-social than to oppose any action which causes any harm to anyone. … It is all a question of weighing up the gains that would accrue from eliminating these harmful effects against the gains that accrue from allowing them to continue." {Coase 1960} Economist Walter Block and others object to the Coase Theorem by pointing out that initial and subsequent allocation of property rights cannot be untwined from efficiency and certainly not from justice, and thus from policy push-back. {Cordato 2007}

An obvious area of property rights **application** is natural resources and the environment. A leader in this from the John Locke Foundation, Roy Cordato, advocates that: "[T]he only practical solution to conflicts that arise over the economic aspects of these otherwise non-economic resources is private property". This is because: "[I]f the defining characteristic of pollution is that it is the consequence of a human conflict over the use of a resource, then it is logical that both the origin and the solution of the problem is to be found in a lack of clearly defined or enforced property rights." {Cordato 2007} A less obvious application is investment sovereign risk or regime uncertainty. A pioneer in this from the Independent Institute, Dr Robert Higgs, describes it thusly: "By this, I mean a pervasive lack of confidence among investors in their ability to foresee the extent to which future government actions will alter their private property rights." {Higgs 1997}

References:

- Adam Smith, *An Inquiry into the Nature and Causes of The Wealth of Nations*, 1776

- Armen Alchian, *Property Rights*, 2008

- Black's Law Dictionary, http://thelawdictionary.org/, 2017

- Claude Frédéric Bastiat, *The Law*, 1853

- Friedrich von Hayek, *The Pretence of Knowledge*, 1974

- Murray Rothbard, *Justice and Property Rights: The Failure of Utilitarianism*, 1973

- Murray Rothbard, *Power and Market: Government and the Economy*, 1977

- Robert Higgs, *Regime Uncertainty: Why the Great Depression Lasted So Long and Why Prosperity Resumed after the War*, 1997

- Ronald Coase, *The Problem of Social Cost*, 1960

- Roy Cordato, *Toward an Austrian Theory of Environmental Economics*, 2007

10. Hands off the Internet (the digital economy abhors regulation)

The modern Internet is the ultimate expression of free people and free markets.

The **Internet** is "the single worldwide computer network that interconnects other computer networks, on which end-user services, such as World Wide Web sites or data archives, are located, enabling data and other information to be exchanged" and "all of which use the same set of communication protocols". {Dictionary.com website} Much of this interconnected network uses old and new telecommunications assets. Telecommunications is about the sharing of information over a distance, including data, text, pictures, voice, and video. Both telecommunications and information technology assets consist of both electronic hardware and computing software, and usually involve the following elements: information creation; information conversion or modulation; information transmission; information carriage, including possibly boosting and further conversion; information reception; information conversion or demodulation; and information absorption. Information, in the form of electromagnetic radiation, is what is always being transmitted on networks like the Internet.

Economically, **networks** like the Internet use a multiple of component services to deliver the overall network service. Interestingly, these component services are complementary in respect of each other but often have close substitutes that could be integrated into the network instead. Economically, information is costly to produce but cheap to reproduce or, in other words, production of an information good involves high fixed costs but low variable costs. Information goods are experience goods – ie a good consumers must experience in order to value it. Many economists and competition regulators, particularly in the early years of the privatised and commercialised Internet, were concerned about: complementarity, including compatibility, standards and systems competition; lock-in and switching costs, including recognising and managing it; and, especially, network externalities and standards, including standards cooperation versus standards war. (see Economides 1996, Shapiro & Varian 1999 and Shy 2001) Regarding the latter, when the value of a product to one user depends on how many other users there are, then this product exhibits network externalities. Technologies subject to strong network effects tend to exhibit long lead times followed by explosive growth. The pattern results from positive feedback – ie as the installed base of users grows, more and more users find adoption worthwhile. Eventually, the product achieves critical mass and takes over the market. Regulation advocates of all stripes are always concerned about, and on the look-out for, so called market failures like externalities.

Senior fellows at the Discovery Institute, Hance Haney and George Gilder, remind that Internet related **regulation** has been around for a long time: "Since the Great Depression, the telecom industry has been subject to comprehensive regulation, with the Federal Communications Commission (FCC) in charge of interstate services and state public utility commissions [PUCs] overseeing intrastate services. ... Telephone, cable television, and Internet access are the three major components of the telecom industry." But, yet: "The traditional rationale for utility regulation – that telephone and cable services are natural monopolies – is gone. Continued utility regulation – except as may be necessary for ensuring interconnectivity and number portability – is unnecessary and distorts competition in ways that harm consumers. So far, few states have faced up to this challenge." This was reinforced by regulatory economist and former regulator Alfred Kahn, who said: "[W]herever there is effective competition – typically and most powerfully, between competing platforms, landline telephony, cable and wireless – regulation of the historical variety is both unnecessary and likely to be anti-competitive." In the wake of this, Haney and Gilder advocate that: "[P]olicymakers should undertake regulatory reform … to attract new investment to the telecom sector so phone, cable, and Internet consumers can receive the services they want at competitive prices." They also add that: "[Greater] investment [would] be a powerful generator of new jobs and economic growth. A study by the Brookings Institution found 'for every one percentage point increase in broadband penetration in a state, employment is projected to increase by 0.2 to 0.3% per year'." {Haney & Gilder 2009}

There are also new regulations on the horizon for the Internet, as pointed out by Susan Dudley and Jerry Brito of the Regulatory Studies Center at George Washington University: "Most notably, the FCC has adopted net **neutrality** rules to prevent Internet service providers from using market power to unreasonably discriminate among data traffic on their networks. Other regulatory efforts have addressed privacy, cybersecurity, and piracy." {Dudley & Brito 2012} Haney and Gilder expand on the former as follows: "'Network neutrality' is a somewhat-flexible label given to … regulations that would prevent network providers from offering deals to one content provider unless they offer the same deal to all providers." And this would be: "[T]he opposite of the pricing flexibility and freedom to innovate that is required to encourage and reward new investment in telecom services and infrastructure." This would cause: "[M]any investors to stay on the sidelines, as occurred in the cable industry following reregulation in 1992 and the phone industry following passage of the regulation-laden *1996 Telecommunications Act*. In both cases, telecom investment crashed when investors saw that new rules would undermine expected returns on new investments." Also: "By deterring product differentiation, net neutrality regulation could easily have the perverse effect of limiting or even destroying competition. Homogeneity imposed by regulation, in other words, could lead us back to monopoly." Therefore: "By embracing regulatory reform, legislators can expand customer choice, decrease prices, and ignite the broadband expansion necessary to economic growth and technological progress." {Haney & Gilder 2009}

Cause-and-effect doesn't just flow from regulation to the Internet, but also in the opposite direction according to Dudley and Brito: "The emergence of the Internet and electronic rulemaking dockets are changing the dynamics of the regulatory process. Regulation is no longer solely the purview of Washington-based lobbyists. Members of the public now have more opportunities to engage in the regulatory debate ... with the potential for making regulators and regulations more **accountable** to the people." Additionally: "[S]ocial media and other Internet technologies lower the cost of group formation and collective action so that citizens will be better able to educate themselves about the regulations that affect them and to take action to make their voices heard." {Dudley & Brito 2012}

A lightly or non-regulated Internet may have an even larger economic and social significance than so far discussed. As entrepreneurism economist Peter Klein put it: "[T]he Internet [is] a case in point that liberty is the mother of **innovation**" because "[i]t is only thanks to market participants that the Internet became something other than a typical government program, characterized by inefficiency, overcapitalization, and irrelevance." And: "Of course, almost all of the Internet's current applications – unforeseen by its original designers – have been developed in the private sector." He does give government its due however: "We must be very careful not to describe the Internet as a private technology, a spontaneous order, or a shining example of capitalistic ingenuity ... [as] yes, the government was the founder of the Internet." But: "As a result, we are left with a panoply of lingering inefficiencies, misallocations, abuses, and political favoritism." Plus: "[Many] Internet enthusiasts tend to forget the fallacy of the broken window. We see the Internet. We see its uses. We see the benefits it brings. ... But we will never see the technologies that weren't developed because the resources that would have been used to develop them were confiscated by the Defense Department and given to Stanford engineers." Moving on, he warned about Internet regulations like network neutrality which he described as "a form of network socialism that can only stymie the Internet's continued growth and development". "Of course, Federal, state, and local governments can own broadband lines as they own streets and highways, or they can treat network infrastructure as a regulated public utility." But: "Any resource the government controls will be allocated based on political priorities." And hence, in conclusion: "[Continuing] government involvement accounts for the Internet's continuing problems, while the market should get the credit for its glories." {Klein 2010}

Publisher and entrepreneur Jeffrey Tucker, of *Liberty.me* and the Foundation for Economic Education, highlights the Internet: "[A] s a **spontaneous-order**, extended constantly by people's desire to know and connect. It is the most poignant and beautiful example in our midst of the capacity of people to organize their lives on their own, with the assistance of merchants, coders, promoters, entrepreneurs, and property holders." Also, he says: "[N]o one person can possibly comprehend the extent, structure, or direction of this order that is emerging in our time. The knowledge that makes it possible is decentralized among billions of users themselves, each of whom grasps only the discrete choices that he or she is making at any one instant." This means that: "The political implications have yet to dawn on this generation ... [including] the illusion that our analog-age governments can make any kind of positive [regulatory] contribution to [this] future." It also means that: "Digital spaces [have] unleashed humankind's creative energy when the masters of the [regulatory] world had almost killed it off." {Tucker 2014} Actuary Gennady Stolyarov like Tucker, is most positive looking forward: "As a decentralized communication system facilitating the sending and receiving of messages by billions of people, the Internet has greatly shifted the balance of power away from governments and toward sovereign individuals." {Stolyarov 2008}

The Internet has many strong parallels with Hayek's views of free and competitive markets as a **discovery-process**. Monetary economist Jesús Huerta de Soto summarizes some of these views as follows: "The essence of [this] social process lies in the strictly personal, subjective, practical and dispersed information or knowledge which every person, in their particular circumstances of time and place, gradually discovers and generates with each one of the human actions they undertake in order to achieve their particular ends and objectives." Therefore: "For people to be able to entrepreneurially discover and transmit the huge volume of practical information or knowledge which the advancement and preservation of today's civilization require, it must be possible for them to freely conceive ends and discover the means necessary to accomplish them, without any sort of hindrance, especially systematic or institutional coercion or force [like regulation]." {de Soto 2008}

References:

- Carl Shapiro & Hal Varian, *Information Rules: A Strategic Guide to the Network Economy*, 1999

- Dictionary.com & Thesaurus.com, http://www.dictionary.com/ & http://www.thesaurus.com/, 2017

- Gennady Stolyarov, *Liberation by Internet: How Technology Destroys Tyranny*, 2008

- Hance Haney & George Gilder, *Ten Principles Of Telecom Policy*, 2009

- Jeffrey Tucker, *Liberty.me: Freedom Is a Do-It-Yourself Project*, 2014

- Jesús Huerta de Soto, *The Austrian School: Market Order and Entrepreneurial Creativity*, 2008

- Nicholas Economides, *The Economics of Networks*, 1996

- Oz Shy, *The Economics of Network Industries*, 2001

- Peter Klein, *The Capitalist and the Entrepreneur: Essays on Organizations and Markets*, 2010

- Susan Dudley & Jerry Brito, *Regulation: A Primer*, 2012

Conclusion

"Standing in the middle of the road is very dangerous; you get knocked down by the traffic from both sides."

– Prime Minister Margaret Thatcher

The case for regulation reform, especially deregulation, is very strong indeed. This can be properly guided by these *Ten Principles of Regulation and Reform*. But unlike in other areas of government intervention, there is much more work needed to be done in regulation and reform, both practical and conceptual. To quote Dr Robert Bradley: "The economics and politics of [regulation] is a fertile field for social science research." {Bradley 2003} But of course, as mathematician and economist John Maynard Keynes once warned: "The difficulty lies not so much in developing new ideas as in escaping from old ones." {Keynes 1936} These *Ten Principles* should therefore assist in escaping from the bad old ideas that never seem to go away.

In terms of the **tools** of better/smarter regulation and deregulation, the PC has identified many frameworks, approaches, tools, etc that could serve as benchmarks and ideas for regulatory reforms including: appeal mechanisms; benchmarking; business burden budgets and trading; business surveys and focus groups; consultation and eDemocracy; disallowable instruments; economic modelling and counterfactuals; 'one-in one-out' type rules; reduction targets; reviews – eg *ex ante* v *ex post*, in-depth, post implementation, principles-based, stocktake, triggered, etc; sunsetting; and standard cost modelling. {PC website} The Mercatus Center identified several criteria for effective regulatory reform, based on US historical experience with previous such reforms – ie: "Independent oversight"; "Veto power"; "Broad applicability"; and "Expert oversight." And based on these, Mercatus found that: "[T]he creation of the Congressional Office of Regulatory Affairs and particularly the *Regulatory Accountability Act*, score well across all criteria." {Abdukadirov 2014}

It shouldn't need reminding, but often does, that by far and away the best source of information on both the regulation problem and the regulation reform solution are **businesses**. This should include their representative bodies, but not to the exclusion of the actual businesses themselves, and particularly the entrepreneurs and risk-takers, even more so than the managers and passive investors. A good way to gather such information is through regular and well thought out opinion surveys, but not to the exclusion of actual conversations with the businesses themselves. A good example of this was a CEO-level survey conducted by Wisconsin Manufacturers and Commerce (WMC) in 2010-11 of small, medium and large businesses throughout most state based industries. This survey was mainly about regulatory burdens but also included a question about preferences for the following regulatory reforms: "Add a sunset provision to new regulations"; "Enact a moratorium on adopting new regulations"; "Enhance due process/ability to challenge agency rules and decisions"; "Establish the Commerce Department as the central business permitting agency"; "Periodic audit/needs assessment for all regulations"; "Require a cost/benefit justification for new or revised regulations"; "Require state regulations to strictly conform to corresponding federal standards"; "Require the Governor and/or Legislature to approve agency rules prior to adoption". {WMC website}

More important still is the sound **economics** that prompts, informs and sustains real reforms. Sound economics includes better understanding regulation life cycles. Milton Friedman nicely illustrated the typical one, albeit one usually without 'death', that many regulations go through: "A real or fancied evil leads to demands to do something about it. A political coalition forms consisting of sincere, high-minded reformers and equally sincere interested parties [ie baptists and bootleggers]. The incompatible objectives of the members of the coalition (eg low prices to consumers and high prices to producers) are glossed over by fine rhetoric about the public interest, fair competition, and the like. The coalition succeeds in getting [government] to pass a law [or regulation]. The preamble to the law [or regulation] pays lip service to the rhetoric and the body of the law [or regulation] grants power to government officials to 'do something'. The high-minded reformers experience a glow of triumph and turn their attention to new causes. The interested parties go to work to make sure that the power is used for their benefit. They generally succeed. Success breeds its problems, which are met by broadening the scope of intervention. Bureaucracy takes its toll so that even the initial special interests no longer benefit. In the end the effects are precisely the opposite of the objectives of the reformers and generally do not even achieve the objectives of the special interests. Yet the activity is so firmly established and so many vested interests are connected with it that repeal of the initial legislation [or regulation] is nearly inconceivable. Instead, new government legislation [or regulation] is called for to cope with the problems produced by the earlier legislation [or regulation] and a new cycle begins." {Friedman 1979}

In terms of the political **strategy** and tactics of reform, president of the Mises Institute Llewellyn Rockwell noted: "Ultimately you must frame your arguments in terms of what is good for the state, and the reality is that [less government] is not usually good for the state. ... The state is open to persuasion, to be sure, but it usually acts out of fear, not friendship. If the bureaucrats and politicians fear backlash, they will not increase taxes or regulations. If they sense a high enough degree of public outrage, they will even repeal controls and programs. An example is the end of alcohol prohibition or the repeal of the 55 mph speed limit. These were pulled back because politicians and bureaucrats sensed too high a cost from continued enforcement." {Rockwell 2008}

It has been said that "those who do not learn from history are doomed to repeat it" and that "there is nothing new in the world except the history you don't know". Thus, in terms of the future **prospects** for reform, Murray Rothbard reminded that, in many ways, the history of humanity can be seen as a race between bigger government versus freer markets, including more versus less regulation: "Always man – led by the producers – has tried to advance the conquest of his natural environment. And always men – other men – have tried to extend political power in order to seize the fruits of this conquest over nature. … In the more abundant periods, eg after the Industrial Revolution, [freer markets took] a large spurt ahead of political power [including over regulation], which ha[d] not yet had a chance to catch up. The stagnant periods are those in which [such] power has at last come to extend its control over the newer areas of [freer markets]." {Rothbard 1977}

References:

- John Maynard Keynes, *The General Theory of Employment, Interest and Money*, 1936

- Llewellyn Rockwell, *The Left, the Right, and the State*, 2008

- Milton Friedman, *Free To Choose: A Personal Statement*, 1979

- Murray Rothbard, *Power and Market: Government and the Economy*, 1977

- Productivity Commission, http://www.pc.gov.au/research/supporting/regulation-taskforce, 2006

- Robert Bradley, *A Typology of Interventionist Dynamics*, 2003

- Sherzod Abdukadirov, *Evaluating Regulatory Reforms: Lessons for Future Reforms*, 2014

- Wisconsin Manufacturers and Commerce, https://www.wmc.org/news/press-releases/common-sense-regulation-reforms-will-improve-business-climate/, 2011

Appendices

A. Regulation Economics 101

"The drivers of the high and rising cost-of-living in Australia are all the plethora of government interventions that, not only increasingly skew the balance of freedom versus control away from freedom, but also necessarily raise costs and prices and thus reduce growth and jobs. Key amongst these government drivers are tax, regulation and money. And key amongst the negative impacts are in energy, housing and banking." – Darren Brady Nelson

The high and rising cost-of-living in Australia, the USA and most everywhere else on this planet, now and throughout civilised history, is a **government** phenomenon. In attempting to answer the question of "why is it so?", the logic of why free markets are economically and ethically good and hence why 'Big Government' interventions of tax, regulation and money are bad will be stepped through. The steps taken are: people; profits; property; prices; and purchasing-power. As will be seen, purchasing-power is the inverse of the cost-of-living. {Nelson 2017}

Economics is about human action – ie **people** acting through time and space in pursuit of ends using means, none of which are infinite or free and thus are of value. All people are individual human beings, but who necessarily interact and cooperate with others such as family, friends, employers/employees and service-providers. The late great historian and sociologist Franz Oppenheimer pointed out that:

> *"[Th]ere are fundamentally two ways [or means] of satisfying a*

person's wants [or ends]: (1) by production and voluntary exchange with others on the market; and (2) by violent expropriation of the wealth of others. The first method is the 'economic' means for the satisfaction of wants; the second method is the 'political' means. The State is trenchantly defined as the organization of the 'political' means. {Oppenheimer 1926}

The outcome sought by all human action is **profit** – ie the ends achieved were worth the means including time and effort. Such profits can be any combination of monetary, material and 'psychic'. For example, if I buy a coffee from a café then by definition I valued it at some level above the exchange price and at the same time the café valued it at some level below the price. Both of us profit – ie I get a consumer surplus and they get a producer surplus. This is by definition 'win-win', at least ex ante. This means that profits, even monetary ones, are not at the expense of other people like consumers or employees. But instead profits provide the incentives and information for entrepreneurs to provide goods and services plus jobs that wouldn't otherwise be provided. Therefore, the statist cliché of "people before profits" is really saying "(my) profits before (other) people".

Private **property** allows for the peaceful pursuit of profit (= ends - means) in cooperation with others, often countless others around-the-world. Property is so much more than just a 'legal' right to own and control land or so called 'real' property. It is the 'natural' right to have the freedom to own and control oneself (including ends), one's stuff (including means) and one's life (including profits) in differentiation from other people. In terms of the economics of private property, the great Austrian School philosopher Hans-Hermann Hoppe said:

"[P]rivate property ... produces a higher general standard-of-living than any other one ... [b]ut ultimately ... such considerations can only convince somebody of [private property] who has already accepted the 'utilitarian' goal of general wealth maximization." {Hoppe 1993}

More importantly, in terms of the ethics of private property, Hoppe said:

> *"[A] property right to one's own body must be said to be justified a priori, for anyone who tried to justify any norm whatsoever would already have to presuppose the exclusive right of control over [one's own] body as a valid norm simply in order to say 'I propose such and such'."*

> *"Furthermore, it would be equally impossible to sustain [such] argumentation for any length of time ... if one were not allowed to appropriate in addition to one's body other scarce means ... For if no one had the right to control anything at all except [one's] own body, then we would all cease to exist ..."* {Hoppe 1993}

Prices are the key contractual term in any exchange of property whether it is say money for coffee, barter for coffee or labour for coffee. Prices at the same time are an objective benchmark, along with objective quantities and semi-objective qualities of goods and services, for comparison to subjective value. Thus prices, like profits, are incentives and information intertwined. Prices, however, can be known ex ante and profits, although expected ex ante, can only be known ex post. Furthermore, because value is subjective in the 'eye of the beholder', it is possible for two people to exchange some of their property at the one price and both 'walk away' with the 'more valuable' item. Hence voluntary exchange is always 'win-win', at least ex ante. As the late great Austrian School economist Friedrich von Hayek added:

> *"Into the determination of ... prices there will enter the effects of particular information possessed by every one of the participants in the market process—a sum of facts which in their totality cannot be known to the scientific observer, or to any other single brain ... which [instead] exists only dispersed among uncounted persons, [more] than any one person can possess."* {Hayek 1974}

This brings us to **purchasing-power**, be it for consumers or businesses. As another late great Austrian School economist Murray Rothbard stated:

> *"The price and purchasing power of the unit of a product are one and the same. .... While recognizing the extreme difficulty of arriving at a measure, it should be clear conceptually that ... the purchasing power of is the inverse of whatever we can construct as the price level or the level of overall prices. In mathematical terms: PPM = 1/P; where PPM is the purchasing power of [money] and P is the price level."* {Rothbard 1983} (see the graph below)

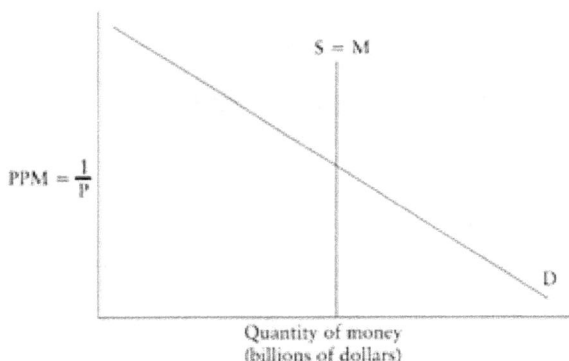

PPM = $\frac{1}{P}$

S = M

D

Quantity of money
(billions of dollars)

When purchasing-power decreases ... say due to an increase in tax, regulation and/or money ... this means that **cost-of-living** increases. Unlike tax and regulation (even income tax or energy regulation), increasing or inflating the money supply impacts on the entire economy over time as: 1) the boom-bust 'business' cycle, reflected in higher prices (and higher profits) for some in the boom; and 2) ultimately 'inflation', reflected in higher prices (and lower profits) for most if not all. By the way, tax and regulation put upwards pressure on prices and downwards pressure on purchasing-power ... not through increased demand for goods and services like money does ... but through decreased supply for goods and services. Rothbard illustrates what happens to purchasing-power of money (PPM) when money supply (M) is inflated:

> *"Having too much money 'burning a hole' in their pockets, people spend the [extra] cash balances, thereby raising individual demand curves and driving up prices. But as prices rise, people find that their increased aggregate of cash balances is getting less and less excessive, since more and more cash is now needed to accommodate the higher price levels."* {Rothbard 1983} (see the graph below)

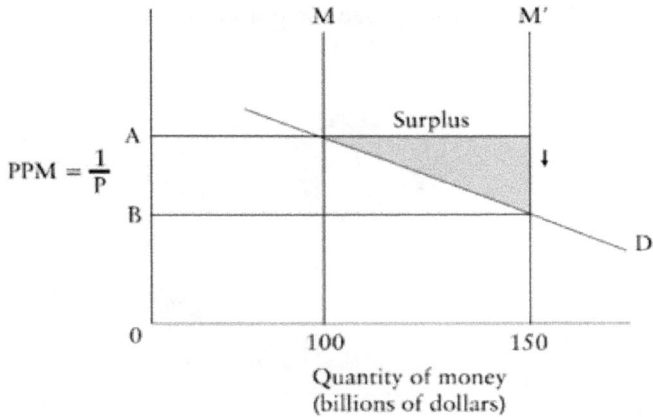

All government policies either: A) reduce or remove market interventions; or B) add to them. "A" reduces the cost-of-living, whilst "B" raises it. To **win** this 'race' over time for 'freer markets' will require not only winning 'minds' through sound economics but also 'hearts' through sound 'ethics' … and maybe sadly 'wallets' through buying off cronies (eg taxis), threatening governments (eg secession) and/or bypassing cronies & governments (eg Uber). {Nelson 2017}

References:

- Darren Brady Nelson, *The Rising Cost-of-Living: Why Is It So?*, 2017

- Franz Oppenheimer, *The State: Its History and Development Viewed*

Sociologically, 1926

- Friedrich von Hayek, *The Pretence of Knowledge*, 1974

- Hans-Hermann Hoppe, *The Economics and Ethics of Private Property*, 1993

- Murray Rothbard, *Power and Market: Government and the Economy*, 1977

- Murray Rothbard, *The Mystery of Banking*, 1983

B. Regulation Dynamics Typology

"Paraphrasing the late great Austrian economist Murray Rothbard, the catch-22 for the advocates of government intervention over liberty is that: they cannot assume that consenting adults in free markets are akin to ignorant and selfish children, but also assume these same people are magically no longer ignorant and selfish when either voting for, or employed by, government." – Darren Brady Nelson

Dr Robert Bradley provides valuable insights into the size and growth of regulation as well as reform including deregulation. His dynamic theory provides a process typology that builds upon some of the economic greats of the 20th century including Friedman, Hayek, Mises and Rothbard. Also in terms of the conceptual side of regulation and interaction with markets, he provides a very useful 'jumping off point' for future research on the economics of regulation and reform.

Part of Dr Bradley's theory is worth quoting here at some length as it also helps to offer a modern and sweeping framework that to a significant extent encompasses the others, and "can be employed for prediction *ex ante* or historical analysis *ex post*". {Bradley 2003}

> *"The primary impetus for an intervention into the market economy [eg regulation] may be external or internal. An external intervention is one that is imposed on a firm, firms, or industry from political-sector reformers. The intervention may have some industry support, but such support is secondary to the purely political momentum for the intervention. The political impetus could be from general voter sentiment, academic research, or lobbying by influential groups so long as the effort is not primarily associated with industry. An internal intervention is driven by vested business lobbying. Such interventions would not have been enacted by reformers alone without such well*

defined support. Interventions that were originally driven externally may come to be internally supported. Six categories of internal intervention can be presented: 1) Self-horizontal intervention where a regulation is obtained by the firm(s) for all members in its industry for its (their) competitive advantage. 2) Vertical intervention in which the firm(s) obtain(s) regulation of upstream suppliers or downstream customers for competitive advantage. 3) Horizontal intervention where a regulation is secured by the instigating firm(s) for competitive advantage over rival firms. 4) Inter-industry intervention where a regulation is obtained by the firm(s) in one industry for a firm or firms in another industry for competitive advantage. 5) Self-intervention where a regulation is obtained by the instigating firm(s) for itself (themselves) but not its competitors. 6) Self-vertical intervention where a regulation is obtained for competitive advantage by a firm(s) for itself (themselves) and for upstream suppliers or downstream customers for competitive advantage."

"Regulators by the force of their personality and skill can propel the cumulative process [of regulation] toward more or less interventionism. [Seven] categories are identified: 1) Professional regulator, who welcomes activism as a way of life and public calling. 2) Naïve idealist, whose good intentions toward the powers at hand may be marred by negative experiences and even disillusionment, but he or she soldiers on. 3) Opportunist, who sees interventionism as a means to greater ends of power, income and prestige. 4) Pro-industry regulator, who combines a propensity to regulate with a bias for the regulated industry. 5) Anti-industry regulator, who combines a preference for regulation with a bias against the regulated industry. 6) Pragmatic regulator, who unlike the opportunist is not wed to the powers at hand but becomes indoctrinated toward regulatory activism. 7) Pro-market regulator who works to minimize his or her authority and permitted responsibilities to allow greater scope for market forces. These classifications can change over time with any particular individual. A regulator could be a blend of the above 'ideal types'."

Dr Bradley's *Typology of Interventionist Dynamics* is worth quoting again here at some length as it also helps to offer a modern and sweeping framework that to a significant extent encompasses the others just mentioned, and "can be employed for prediction *ex ante* or historical analysis *ex post*". {Bradley 2003}

> *"Three classifications can capture and qualitatively describe virtually all interventions in a market: dormant vs. causal; non-initiating vs. initiating; and initiating vs. consequent (cumulative). The interrelationships of each are illustrated [below]. Causal intervention impacts the decision-making of market participants. A non-initiating intervention is one that does not engender subsequent intervention. An initiating intervention spawns further intervention into the economy. In all cases, the ensuing intervention can be traced back to the initiating intervention, which by definition is also a causal intervention."*

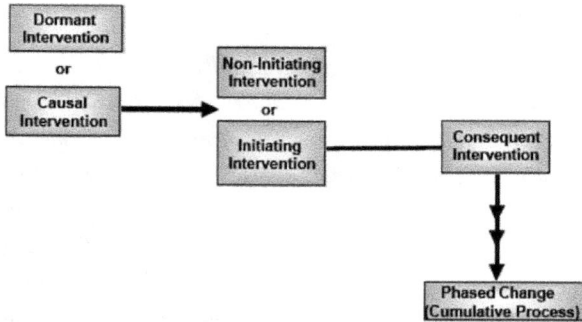

> *"An interventionist regulation therefrom can be expansionary, contractionary, or both at any point in the cumulative process [see below]. Consequent [expansionary] intervention can be divided into phases. The chronological sequence can occur over a short or long time sequence and involve new jurisdictions. Deregulation or [contractionary intervention] is an unwinding process that can occur incrementally with the removal of cumulative expansions or totally with the repeal of the initiating intervention upon which the cumulative intervention rests. Incremental [deregulation] is unlikely to 'play the tape in reverse'. More likely, the [deregulation] path*

will occur in fewer steps than the expansion did – and maybe in just one step. Cumulative intervention can contain many threads of intervention and dis-intervention. Judgment is necessary amid the myriad regulatory provisions to determine whether the overall effect represents less or more intervention than before – and whether [a reform] creates more or less momentum toward (de)regulation in the future. The cumulative process is temporally sequential in the large majority of cases as one intervention gives impetus to the next. But there can be instances of interventions being related after an interim non-interventionist period."

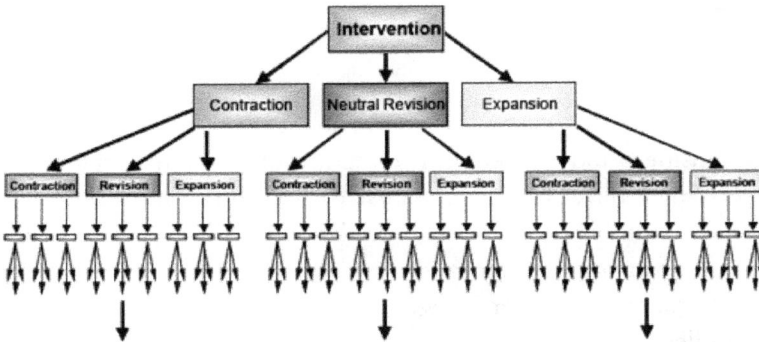

"The range of possibilities and special cases mirrors the panoply of subjective, causal motivations driving the interventionist process. Accordingly, the different categories of this dynamic typology are qualitative, making historical judgment necessary to identify initial categories and evaluate linkages as strong or weak, direct or indirect, sequential or intermittent, microeconomic or also macroeconomic, and regional, national or international. There cannot be a quantitative typology because interventionist dynamics, like the entrepreneurial process elsewhere, is purposeful human action."

References:

- Robert Bradley, *A Typology of Interventionist Dynamics*, 2003

C. Infrastructure Regulation Unwarranted

"The very term public utility ... is an absurd one. Every good is useful to the public, and almost every good, if we take a large enough chunk of supply as the unit, may be considered necessary. Any designation of a few industries as public utilities is completely arbitrary and unjustified."
– Murray Rothbard

Every business and household is directly and indirectly impacted by the seemingly never-ending rise in **infrastructure** prices (including airports, electricity, gas, post, public transport, rail, seaports, telecommunications, water and sewerage ... often called public utilities). State and federal regulation of these so called natural monopolies (very worryingly, possibly including the Internet), in fact, virtually locks in such an upward trajectory. Consequently, consumers are paying a pseudo-tax that is hidden in plain sight. {Nelson 2015} This is in great part due to, as pointed out by economist Ludwig von Mises, that: "No alleged fact finding and no armchair speculation can discover another price at which demand and supply would become equal. The failure of all experiments to find a satisfactory solution for the limited-space monopoly of public utilities clearly proves this truth." {Mises 1949}

Almost everyone outside the world of Austrian economics, including establishment free-market economists, unquestionably assumes the need for public utility regulation. This is, to borrow a buzz-word from the Left, unsustainable in both theory and practice, as evidenced by the following Ten **Catch-22s** of public infrastructure utilities:

#1 Monopolies are unnatural (not natural)

#2 Markets are undefinable (not defined)

#3 Competition is a process (not a structure)

#4 Value is subjective (not objective)

#5 Prices determine costs (not vice versa)

#6 Weighted average cost of capital as interest and return (not)

#7 Incentives are profits and losses (not formulas and benchmarks)

#8 Information is created and decentralised (not given and centralised)

#9 Regulation hasn't worked (in practice)

#10 Regulation can't work (in theory)

These Ten Catch-22s can be put in the **context** of the orthodox framework of industrial organisation economics as follows (which is a subset of Neoclassical economics and by-and-large the basis for regulatory economics): #1 #2 #3 are market structure related; #4 #5 are market conduct related; #6 #7 #8 are market performance related; and #9 #10 are market intervention related. Structure and conduct are supposed to help address why, where and when there should be regulation. Conduct and performance are supposed to help address what and how to regulate. Intervention is supposed to help address if regulation can (positively or negatively) impact the other areas … usually assuming, unwisely, that regulation had no negative impact previously, and that regardless it can still impact positively going forward. {Hirshleifer 2005}

Orthodox economic theories on the market failure of natural **monopoly** versus perfect competition (along with competition policy and antitrust law approaches to market definition) provide most of the rationale for heavy handed (price, service, etc) regulation of utilities, starting with standard economic theories of market structure. Even though many establishment economists acknowledge that natural monopoly and perfect competition are blackboard ideals, at the end of the day they are still the benchmarks for whether to regulate or not … and to continue to do so, or not. In both Austrian economics theory and real world practice, markets are just a convenient and aggregated description of the constant flux of exchange opportunities created and discovered by suppliers and consumers with skin-in-the-game. And, of course, defining a market narrowly enough will always yield market power; defining a market broadly enough may always yield perfect competition thus a market cannot be independently established as such apart from consumer preference on the market.

As to perfect competition, perhaps economics Nobel Laureate Friedrich von Hayek said it best: "[C]ompetition is by its nature a dynamic process whose essential characteristics are assumed away by the assumptions underlying static analysis" thus "perfect competition means indeed the absence of all competitive activities." {Hayek 1947} More importantly, the little known history of natural monopoly (in the USA, at least) teaches that there was plenty of effective competition (and its attendant decreasing costs and prices, and increasing quantity, quality, service and innovation) prior to the less effective competitors lobbying for market protection regulation in exchange for utility oversight regulation. In fact, the regulation of natural monopolies started well before the theory of natural monopoly. Plus, if a utility monopoly were natural (ie could produce at a lower total cost than all others, actual and potential) it would not be in need of all of the other types of regulations (intentionally and unintentionally) preventing market entry.

All the different approaches to market conduct under utility regulation are all founded on the (explicit or at least implicit) assumption that **value** (particularly costs) are objective and that they do (or should) determine prices. Firstly, costs are prices too, just from another's point of view. Secondly, causation largely flows the opposite way from prices to costs, not costs to prices. Thirdly, all values (that determine opportunity costs and prices through exchange) are subjective not objective. Fourthly, pricing and other value related decisions are made at the margin … margin meaning what happens next, not necessarily one additional unit of output and certainly not an infinitesimal change as per the calculus. All of this was established by one of the founding fathers of the marginal revolution in economics (for both Austrian and Neoclassical Schools), Carl Menger, who said:

"Value is … nothing inherent in goods, no property of them. Value is a judgment economizing men make about the importance of the goods at their disposal for the maintenance of their lives and well-being. Hence value does not exist outside the consciousness of men." {Menger 1871} Another way of putting this is: "Marx would say pearls have value because people dive for them (thus supplying labor). Menger would retort that people dive for pearls because people value them." {Baker 2007} It is also worth noting that in real world free markets, prices are determined in exchange by Eugen von Böhm-Bawerk's marginal pairs, often between extremely narrow margins. {Böhm-Bawerk 1898}

The regulatory debates in the US (and increasingly in the UK, Australia, NZ, etc) tend to centre around **returns** only. In addition, such return debates outside the US (unlike where broader commercial and fairness factors are more important and explicit) are very much focussed around finance theory rather than finance practice … almost always the weighted average cost of capital (WACC) and the capital asset pricing model (CAPM), plus increasingly financeability. As per Frank Knight (and unlike WACC and CAPM), the real world of free markets is more about dealing with unquantifiable uncertainty rather than semi-quantifiable risk. {Knight 1921} Interest is the less uncertain reward to capitalists (including management), whilst profit is the more uncertain reward to entrepreneurs. It is important to understand that interest is more fundamental than just bank interest on money. As Hayek's contemporary Murray Rothbard said, interest is: "the pure exchange ratio between present and future goods. This rate of return is the rate of interest." Returns are, of course, profits and losses compared to assets and liabilities. Based on this and many other factors, entrepreneurs, savers, investors and others react to this and other information and thus set their expectations going forward for future returns. In this regard, Rothbard stated: "there is no sense whatever in talking of a going rate of profit. … For any realized profit tends to disappear because of the entrepreneurial actions it generates." He importantly added that: "A grave error is made by a host of writers and economists in considering only profits in the economy. Almost no account is taken of losses. ... [from] when an entrepreneur has made a poor estimate of his future." {Rothbard 1962} As for entrepreneurs, Spanish Professor Jesús Huerta de Soto reminds: "Neoclassical theorists view entrepreneurship as an ordinary factor of production which can be allocated depending on expected costs and benefits ... their thinking involves an insoluble logical contradiction: to demand entrepreneurial resources based on their expected costs and benefits entails the belief that one has access today to certain information (the probable value of future costs and benefits) before this information has been created by entrepreneurship itself. ... until this process of creation is complete the information does not exist nor can it be known." {de Soto 2008}

The reason this system of regulation is akin to a tax, is that unlike most other forms of regulation, it regularly produces readily identifiable impacts in the form of the regulated prices that have to be paid directly or indirectly by every business and household in the country. These **pseudo-taxes** are almost always on the rise like real taxes (as per the graph below), and also like the latter include all of the predictable inefficiencies associated with government central planning (ie the government regulators) and government protected cronyism (ie the utilities themselves). There have been few comprehensive empirical studies, but these show a poor performance for utility oversight regulation in terms of high prices (as well as low quantity and quality, poor customer service and innovation, etc). This is not surprising, given the lack of economic and political incentives to do so. Like the Fed which does not control but creates inflation, this regulatory system does not control but creates monopoly prices ... through such mechanisms as entry barriers, competition restrictions and substitution impediments as well as through regulatory capture and other PCT effects. Even more fundamentally, these prices aren't even real prices as such, due to the impossibility of socialist economic calculation. Thus, as Hayek once lectured other economists: "[T]he effects on policy of the more ambitious constructions have not been very fortunate … [due] to a pretense of exact knowledge that is likely to be false." {Hayek 1974}

In light of all this, it seems that is about time that some significant **reform** paths to genuine free markets (or at least more free ones) were more seriously considered in Australia, the USA and elsewhere. Pro competition reforms not only need to take genuine steps in the right direction towards free markets (without offsetting steps backwards, at the same or over time), but should also focus on the main game of removing government's own barriers to competition and market entry … along with its other barriers to buyers and suppliers. Hopefully the gaping theoretical, statistical and historical shortcomings of infrastructure regulation can be put more and more on the radar of the long suffering businesses and households of the Western World. {Nelson 2015}

References:

- Carl Menger, *Principles of Economics*, 1871

- Darren Brady Nelson, *Regulation of Public Utilities as a Pseudo Tax*, 2015

- Eugen von Böhm-Bawerk, *Karl Marx and the Close of His System*, 1898

- Frank Knight, *Risk, Uncertainty and Profit*, 1921

- Friedrich von Hayek, *Individualism and Economic Order*, 1947

- Friedrich von Hayek, *The Pretence of Knowledge*, 1974

- Jack Hirshleifer & et al, *Price Theory and Applications*, 2005

- Janice Beecher, *Household Expenditures, Prices and Rate Design for Utility Services: trends and Distributional Effects*, 2015

- Jesús Huerta de Soto, *The Austrian School: Market Order and Entrepreneurial Creativity*, 2008

- Ludwig von Mises, *Human Action: A Treatise on Economics*, 1949

- Murray Rothbard, *Man, Economy and State*, 1962

- Ronald Baker, *Pricing on Purpose: Creating and Capturing Value*, 2007

www.ingramcontent.com/pod-product-compliance
Lightning Source LLC
Chambersburg PA
CBHW031732210326
41519CB00050B/6318